"We Lied to Fire Teacher!"

False Allegations Destroying Teacher Livelihoods

James Curtis Geist

January 2023

"There is no 'teacher shortage.' There are thousands of qualified experienced teachers who are no longer teaching. **There is a shortage of respect and proper compensation for teachers** *to allow them to actually teach."*

-10:02 PM *8/5/22 *Twitter *Jo Lampert@jolambert

2021 Survey: What is the likelihood you will leave teaching?

Unlikely: 46%
Likely: 21%
Very likely: 33%

Devon Karbowski of www.AdoptAClassroom.org

How teaching has changed 2021-22

81%: Workload has increased.
58%: Increase in classroom interruptions during instruction.

www.AdoptAClassroom.org

Dedicated to
my wife,
family,
fellow teachers,
teacher union
representatives &
12 step brothers and sisters
who believed me.

<u>Not dedicated</u>
to the mean girls
who tried to destroy
my teaching career

OTHER BOOKS WRITTEN BY
James Curtis Geist

I. *BIOGRAPHY*
MODERN AUGUSTINIAN CONFESSION:
Memoir of a Minister, Teacher & Activist
(December 2016)

II. *HISTORY*
The Presidents [1-45]
(February 2019)

Global History I, II, III & IV Notes for Teachers *(May 2019)*

United States History Notes for Teachers *(June 2019)*

III. *POETRY AND ANECDOTES*
Bottom of the Food Chain
(June 2017)

Poetry for the Kathy Lee Gifford Child Labor Sweatshop Retirement Village *(October 2017)*

A Robot Ate My Homework:
Poems & Anecdotes for the 4th Revolution Infancy *(December 2017)*

Time Rich & Cash Poor
(May 2018)

Wonder Years of Teenaged Insecurity
(June 2018)

Guns & Butter, Bread & Roses
(July 2018)

Stories of the Helig, Polter & Zeitgeist
Poetry & Anecdotes *(January 2019)*

Ragbag
(March 2019)

Confession: Musings of Mischief
(April 2019)

Moonquakes
(February 2020)

Water Wears the Stones
(February 2021)

Mister Fatty
(May 2022)

IV. CHILDREN'S BOOKS

Jimmy's Summer Beach Camping Trip
(April 2018)
Jimmy's Paper Route
(April 2018)
Jimmy's S-S-S-Summer Experience
(April 2018)
Jimmy's Fishing Trip
(May 2019)
Jimmy's Circus Trip
(May 2019)
Jimmy's Yard Sale
(December 2020)

Jimmy's Snow Day
(December 2020)
Jimmy's Summer Playground
(December 2020)
Jimmy Meets Muhammad Ali
(March 2021)
Jimmy's Summer Family Picnic
(March 2021)

V. *YOUNG ADULT*

Varsity Printing Team
(March 2021)

VI. *COMPILATIONS*

Essential Geist: Volume I & II
Poetry & Anecdotes
(February 2019)

My Canterbury Tale
Poetry & Anecdotes
(March 2019)

Jimmy's Adventures: Volume I
Five Jimmy Stories
(December 2020)

Jimmy's Adventures: Volume II
Five Jimmy Stories
(April 2021)

VII. *RECOVERY – CODEPENDENCE*

Reverend in Recovery
(July 2022)

Changes that have led to an increased need for supplies for students

78%: Learning loss caused by Covid-19

75%: Social emotional learning

65%: Increased workload

54%: Creating a more inclusive classroom

51%: Creating a more culturally-responsive classroom

www.AdoptAClassroom.org

ACCUSATION QUOTES

The false accusation of a person of dubious morality can taint the reputation of an upright person.
-Roman Law

We live and work in a fishbowl, with rumors and accusations flowing constantly.
-Bob Baffert

Accusations and disinformation are weapons used to destroy opposition…
-Will Cain

Lies and accusations are just bullying.
-Mila Kunis

In all moral panics, an accusation is enough to destroy a person's life. Hysteria trumps evidence.
-Carol Tavris

Accusation's are on page one of the newspaper, and retractions on page 19.
-Paul Newman

When you have not basis for an argument, you abuse the plaintiff.
-Cicero

A trial without witnesses, when it involves a criminal accusation, is not a true trial.
-Bill McCollum

An indictment is not a conviction
-Howard Coble

Everybody has a right to be defended, and every lawyer has a duty to defend people accused. My office is to defend by discussing accusations point by point, a normal step in democracy.
     -Jacques Verges

A clear conscience laughs at a false accusation.
     -anonymous

I have much to say why my reputation should be rescued from the load of false accusation which has been heaped upon it.
     -Robert Emmet

Knowledge of God's Word is a bulwark against accusations…
     -Edwin Louis Cole

We must remember always that an accusation is not proof and that conviction depends on evidence and due process of law.
     -Edwin Morrow

One accusation you cannot throw at me is that I have always done my best.

     -Alan Shearer

Geese are friends to no one, they bad mouth everybody and every thing. But, they are companionable once you get used to their ingratitude and false accusations.

     -E.B. White

Percentage of Teachers Falsely Accused

Canada: 13%

United Kingdom: 20%

United States: 22%

Dr. Elizabeth Mae DeLeon (Fall of 2017) &
The Guardian (3-29-15)

TABLE OF CONTENTS

Introduction……..…..…..........……………..…..12

1. The New N.Y.C. Teacher…..…………..……….14

2. Teacher Perfectionism & Codependency……………24

3. Life as a Substitute Teacher……………………...33

4. The Life of a Teacher………………………...…..…..52

5. The Clients - Students…….........................…………..84

6. Teaching Journal - Reflection……………...……......114

7. Bosses……………………………….........………….171

8. Guns, Terrorism, Covid and P.T.S.D……………..…184

9. 9/11/2001 @ Park West High School…………..……241

10. Sexual Harassment……………………………...…..264

11. *FALSE ACCUSTIONS AGAINST TEACHERS…......273

12. Teacher Recovery Quotes & Notes…...............…..…295

Topic Index…..…………….......……………….311

INTRODUCTION:
THANKSGIVING 2022

Thanksgiving for me is the morning drive from northern New Jersey to Pennsylvania to visit Mom, Dad and family. Thanksgiving is the traditional turkey dinner with pumpkin pie and whipped cream, watching football, talking politics with trepidations and a nap from a belly full of food cornucopia and feeling the safety of being with the kin folk.

Whenever I catch the Charlie Brown Thanksgiving Special as a middle-aged step parent, I get choked up. I tear up because I remember sitting in front of the TV as a child at Nana Geist's, or at the home of Grandpa and Nana Short – thankful for the bittersweet memories of loving grandparents now passed on.

For over 20 years, I have always had a fear, some student with a grievance, would make a false accusation against me. This is something I often shared with my family, friends and wife. *That day for me was Wednesday November 16th, 2022, the week before Thanksgiving in my 21st year as a teacher.*

This Thanksgiving morning, I am writing my defense against 6th grade female students making false accusations saying I "body shamed stared at them and touched them." I was informed at a meeting a week earlier by the Principal, with two union representatives at my side the previous day. The resolution meeting is to take place on 11/21/22, however, our Superintendent is killed in a car crash the day before.

The meeting is moved to 11/29 at 10:30 a.m. I know because H.R. sent me an email at 10:47 p.m. the evening before. Luckily I checked my e-mail at 8:30 a.m. Tuesday morning to make the meeting at 10:30 a.m. at a meeting room a one hour commute from my home.

I am so sickened and confused by these false accusations, I tell my parents I will not be attending Thanksgiving with them. I am full of sadness, anger and shame; moreover, my stomach is so twisted, I cannot eat.

As a result of these accusations, my blood pressure is through the roof, I see my doctor who gives me a referral to see a cardiologist to check to make to address possible stroke or a heart attack episode.

On 11/29 at 8:30 a.m., I will be informed in two hours, if I still am a teacher, or if I will be working the following week at Costco. In two hours, I will find out if my four years of college, 3 years of graduate school, and my 20 plus year legacy of teaching, my reputation and my teaching license is about to circle clockwise in the sucking noise of a flushing commode.

Chapter 1
The New N.Y.C. Teacher

"The meaning of life is simple. We are here to learn (Peck, Further Along the Road Less Traveled p. 55).

The 2,000s
On the radio you can hear Train, God Smack, Jane's Addiction, Nickelback, Green Day, the Killers, Foo Fighters, Lady Gaga, the Stone Temple Pilots and the Black Eyed Peas. On television, is Boston Public, Rescue Me, Dirty Jobs, Curb Your Enthusiasm, Malcolm in the Middle and the West Wing. There are hybrid vehicles, You-Tube, Facebook, iPhones and Kindle e-books.

New History Teacher in Hell's Kitchen in NYC
I liked being a teacher. I like being part of the United Federation of Teachers. I liked going to Druids Bar on Fridays. My Assistant Principal was about to retire, he had back pain all the time, and he had no time for me. I had to go to the Bar to get my questions answered by the veteran teachers.

When the A.P. retired, a new one came in. Teachers thought he was nice, but he was not nice to me. He played games with me, I was the only teacher who did not have tenure in the history department. I needed books for one of my classes, and he would not give me the books. Who does that? The kid's parents tax money paid for those books! Mr. Cruz transferred out of the school five years later to become a principle in Cambria Heights Queens.

Shortly thereafter, the Daily News ran a story about the new Bully Principal in Cambria Heights.

I was a dean at the school, and had to fill out paper work when a student was suspended, and had to call parents. I walked the hallways with a walkie-talkie and I enjoyed it.

I once had a young man come into my history class the middle of the school year. He sat in the back of the room, and I asked him where he came from. He said, "Spafford." I asked my union representative what Spafford was. He said it was NYC jail for juvenile delinquents. I asked Franklin why he went to Spafford and he said, "In my last school, I punched out a teacher."

Dating Websites dot com

Now that I was "divorced" and single, I signed up on several dating sights. It was fun, and it was addictive. I went out on many dates. I would walk up to a gorgeous woman and ask her out. What did I have to lose? I once saw a model interviewed and she was asked, "I bet you had plenty of suitors when you were in high school and college." She said, "Actually, I think the guys felt I was unapproachable, so to answer your question is no I did not get asked out on many dates." The worst that could happen is if a potential date said no - I just moved on to the next one.

A problem of living in a City of 10 million people is, I was always looking at the ladies. Pearl Jam has a song called "Better Man," that essentially says, "You are my mate, until I find a better one." This causes anxiety for me. My dating in New York City never developed into anything serious. I guess I did not really want a relationship anyway, since I was planning on moving to West Milford in the summer of 2002.

Why was I attracting women in my life who could not tell me what they were feeling or what they wanted? In hindsight, the people I was attracting into my life were as unhealthy as I was with relationships.

Moving to West Milford N.J.
After Joy moved out, I was tired of living in the City. I wanted to be in the country. I called a real estate agent in West Milford, and over the course of six months, I found a home there. On July 1 of 2002, I moved out of Queens and into my new home in West Milford.

I was happy to have deer, bear, raccoons, coyotes and bear in my backyard. My commute to my NYC job was an hour into the City, and an hour home. I often took the 196 Express Bus, where I could sleep on the way to work and on the way home from work. Jungle Habitat use to abide in West Milford, similar to the Safari Drive at Great Adventure. The bus driver when he stopped at our parking said, "Welcome to West Milford! Watch out for Tigers, Lions and Bears."

Evil is everywhere...
I am so happy to be out of the City. I stop by Three Roads Deli to buy a newspaper on Saturday morning. A man and a woman are walking out a young boy aged three, and the kids screams. Not really my business, I leave.

son at a local deli. I look at the kid with Mohawk, and I recognize him. The father had not reported
it to the police, and I urged him to go to the station soon as church was over. He did report it to police after church.

Workaholism to Run from Guilt of Divorce
I loved my new home. It was built in 1948, and was a home with a stone bottom and pine siding. It looked like a converted hunting cabin. I moved there on July 1st of 2002 to West Milford, and literally worked from sun up to sun down. I felt such guilt getting divorced, and leaving ministry, I worked inside my home, outside my home, and in the 26 acres of woods behind it.

I wish I had sat with my feelings and did the grieving work I needed to do, but all I knew was to stuff the feelings. It was another reason I became a dating maniac, it was just another way of running from feelings. What could be another way to afraid processing sadness and pain? I could run for political office!

The day was coming I would have to pay the emotions piper. My false self was not my friend. My True Self was waiting for me to hit bottom.

Running for Office
I ran for town council in 2006. It was a great experience getting to learn about the issues in our town. Most people in West Milford have septic systems. A few are hooked up
to the water company.

The main issue I ran on was water preservation. West Milford is 80 square miles, and our land provides water for the City of Newark. The minute out town became all
hooked up to a water main, we would have such growth, that our taxes would go through the roof. More people, more schools, more services, higher taxes.

I enjoyed campaigning, getting to meet people, political strategy meetings, and the debates. I drove around town and saw signs that said, "Vote for Geist and Rauth." What an ego boost.

I lost the election, but it was a stressful campaign. I had my car window busted, my tires slashed, and false statements made about me in the newspaper. On the local website, someone was writing scurrilous things about town members in the name of James Geist, but it was not me.

I went to the Sheriff's Office to file a complaint. The Investigation found evidence it was a political operative on the other side. He was arrested for internet impersonation, and then he claimed he was injured when arrested, and I was sued by him in addition to the Sheriff's Office.

He was not jailed or fined, but he spent tens of thousands of dollars for attorney fees for using my name. He thought
it was funny until he was arrested.

It took a year, but his case was finally thrown out. As my friend CarlLa said, the person who started our political
club, "I would rather get stabbed in the eye with a needle,

than run for office again." My town council campaigning experience gives me plenty of stories for my Government Classes.

Love Life of the New York City Teacher

"There is nothing that holds us back more from mental health as a society and God than the sense that many have of unimportance, unloveliness and undesirability"
(Scott Peck, <u>Further Along the Road Less Traveled</u> p 95).

What a Teacher Makes

The dinner guests were sitting around the table discussing life. One man, a C.E.O. decided to explain the problem with education. "What kid is going to learn from a person who became a teacher? Susan, you are a teacher. What do you make?"

Susan, known for her honesty and frankness, paused, then began.

I make kids work harder than they ever thought they could.
I make a C+ student feel like a Congressional Medal winner.
I make kids sit for 55 minutes when parents can't get them to sit for five minutes.
I make them sit five minutes without being on a cell phone.
I make kids wonder.
I make them question.
I make them apologize when they need to.
I make them take responsibility for their actions.
I make them read, read, read.

I help them learn English while preserving their cultural identity.
I elevate them to experience music and art.
I help them understand they have brains and to follow their hearts.
I teach them that if anyone ever tries to judge you the amount of money you make, pay them no attention.

What do I make? I make a difference.

What do you make Mr. C.E.O.?

Breaking My Own Heart

I had a problem of "falling madly in love." As a child, I entertained fantasies and crushes on girls. For me, love was a feeling, not a decision. When I started dating, I found those who could not give me what I wanted. It reinforced the message that I was unlovable and unworthy.

To me, Vanessa, looked like the Dominican version of Sophia Loren. She worked in the medical field, her daughter was in college, and he doctor was smart, spiritual, and even-keeled.

We were friends for 10 years, and when we started dating, I fell hard. We ended up playing house, as I would crash at her place 2-3 times a week. We had dinner, watched a movie, had wine and went to bed. She was my drug.

I was dealing with a boss at work making my life difficult. Secondly, I had a close friend of five years betray my trust.

Thirdly, I was running for a town council seat in my hometown, and the operatives they made false statements about my character. Lastly, I ended up going to court because someone was posting on a local website using my name. Politics is a dirty business.

Long story short, after 8 months, I stopped by her apartment, and she was drinking wine with her "commuter friend." I wanted to take the kitchen knife and stab him in his eye with it. I literally lost my breath. She broke up with me a week later, and I could not let go.

I sent her e-mails, letter, and even stopped by the apartment twice unannounced trying to win my love back. I NEVER would have caused her harm, but if I really cared for her, I would have respected her "no," and moved on.

I made my qualifier my Higher Power.
I had a dependent personality.
I was getting validation from relationships instead of connection with God and the True Self.
I did not love or value me.
I was unable to give anything to the relationship.
I chose partners who were as sick as I.
I chose emotionally unavailable partners as I was.

The person I used for my relief, now became my master. I thought being in this relationship was like drinking pure water, but what I was drinking was salt water, only increasing my thirst, never able to sate my thirst.

The Big Book says I was using the relationship as a drug to avoid facing my insecurity, loneliness, sense of personal worth and inadequacy (74). My pride and willfulness had hidden the yearning of a lonely fearful child…and emptiness that yearned to be fulfilled (81). What I thought was the cure, was the sickness – *the medicine became the poison.*

When I relationship ended, *I was overwhelmed with grief.* I would later learn from Therapist Dr. Roman, my pain was not the loss of the relationship, but a lifetime of stuffed pain and emotions that was bubbling out. For me, *I had 40 years of stuffed feelings and pain.* Vanessa was the angel sent into my life, to crush my heart, and pull the cork out of my inner stuffed pain bottle.

Withdrawal pain is the worst - but there is no other way. *The cave you fear to enter holds the answer*. For me, it was sitting with my feelings and pain, and grieving it all out. It was a process that took place over one year, where I would weep two to three times a week to get ALL MY 40 YEARS OF UNPROCESSED FEELINGS OUT. The pain I thought was killing me, was actually saving my life.

My N.Y.C. Alcoholic Neighbor and his Crackhead Girlfriend

My neighbors often had their weekly fights late Saturday nights, keeping me up, when I had to work the next day as a pastor - a representative of Jesus. I called the police, there was "Law-n-Order" drama for a half hour, and then things quieted down.

SIX MONTHS LATER: It is summer time, I am walking back to the apartment. What I was doing I do not remember; let us say I went to the corner bodega to buy some milk. As I approach the entry steps, I see a woman sitting there smoking a cigarette. It is the lady who likes to smoke crack.

"Hello" I say.
Hello.
I have not seen you in a while.
Yea, I went to prison for six months.
What happened?
The boyfriend and I got in a fight, the cops showed up and I took a swing at a police officer.
SILENCE.
You know who called the police?
I figured it was you - Thank-you.
What?
No, I was out of mind on crack. While I was in jail, I was able to get clean. That call saved my life. Thank you.

Sometimes having boundaries not improve quality of life, but can save a life. Love, owning your power and grace.

Chapter 2

Many Teachers Struggle with Codependency & Perfectionism

WHAT TEACHERS DO

We create materials and search online for engaging lessons.

We produce educational materials such as lessons, assessments and curriculum.

We differentiate lessons and analyze class and homework.

We help fellow teachers.

We document, document, document.

We input endless data.

We attend meetings: P.L.C.s, Pre & Post Observation and faculty meetings.

We respond to lots of parent questions.

We jam and fix the copier.

We stress about standardized testing.

We manage technology.

We manage classes to ensure optimal learning.

We engage in parent-teacher conferences – planned and impromptu.

We pick up trash, clean tables and organize supplies.

We laminate, label and file everything.

We sharpen lots of pencils.

We create behavior reports.

We stop by the store before or after school to purchase supplies.

We distribute report cards.

We help our students.

We promote enthusiasm and interactive learning.

TEACHER PERFECTIONISM
"I am a perfectionist, and it is exhausting."

Perfection is an illusion that is unattainable.

Set realistic goals based on your own wants and needs. Evaluate success not only in terms of what you accomplished, but also in terms of how much you enjoyed the task.

Ask yourself, "Have I set up impossible expectations for myself in this situation?

Confront the fears that may be behind your perfectionism by asking, "What am I afraid of? What is the worst that could happen?"

Old Tapes/False Self

Old tapes are the critical parent in our heads. These are the negative thoughts I have about myself. I will go to meetings, have my daily contact with God and use positive affirmations to overcoming the old tapes.

Many Teachers are Codependent

Causes of Codependency
- when parents do not respond with feeling.
- send messages of do not care
- inconsistent care
- threats and rejection.

We have mirror neurons, monkeys, apes and humans. If no empathy was modeled, it was likely no empathy was to be exhibited. We mimic what is modeled. We are wired to see people as ourselves.

Causes of lack of empathy
  -pain, stress, dysfunction
  -mental illness, poverty, illness, addiction

In the USA, we have "accepted forms" of action such as bingo, lotto, fantasy, exercise, clutter, work, food, religion and computers. Our society is emotionally dishonest.

Codependency is the disease of lost self-hood.
Getting little to no validation as a child, lead to feeling unlovable when we are adults. We end up with a "hole in the soul" syndrome. What do we fill the hole up with?

Codependent children tend to 1) enmesh, 2) become perfectionistic, 3) shut down feelings, 4) ignore wants.

Is there such a thing as too much empathy?
Yes! It is called codependency.

Codependency starts with unhealthy family rules
1) It is not okay to talk about problems.
2) We communicate indirectly.
3) You must be perfect.
4) You must make the family proud.
5) Be serious, not playful.

A best friend, a pastor out on the West Coast, said after his divorce, went to <u>an anger management class</u>. In the class were ten people - one a pastor, <u>the other nine – teachers</u>.

STAGES OF LIFE

Who Am I? [1-20]   It took me to age 44 to figure out who I was….and that is okay.

Climbing the Career Ladder [21-29]   While I was never really comfortable in my own skin, climbing the career ladder in ministry, then as a Social Studies teacher, I was able to keep busy, feel good about doing, but not about being.

There are No Absolutes [30-35]   The only absolute I know of is there is a God, and I am not God.   Spending time studying religion, ethics, theology, history and psychology, I thought I had a pretty good grasp at living life. As a evangelical, getting a divorce pretty much helped me get close to bottom.   The days of ministry are over, no church board will want a divorced leader.

Mid-Life Crisis: Entering the Cave   [36-45]   Having my heart crushed by the woman of my dreams gets me into the cave. Joseph Campbell says, "The cave you fear to enter, holds your answer." Psychologist Carl Jung said, "The only way out of pain, is through the pain." Learning to face problems and pain head on is mature, and the best way to live an emotionally healthy life.

Mid-Life Resolution - The Best Years   [46-50]   Through the rooms, or the 12 step program, I learn to identify feelings and to sit with them instead of running and using addiction as a way to cover those feelings.

I learn to become present, and my relationships with family and friends have become deeper and healthier.

Mellowing: Friends & Privacy are Important [51 on]
Who are you?
I am a son, brother, uncle, teacher, human rights activist, minister and a teacher.
That is not who you are; that is what you do. Are you a human doing or a human being?

I have learned how to be. I do not have to be a workaholic. Today I can sit at home, not do a thing, and not feel guilty about doing nothing and say, "I had a great day."

I have finally do not run from pain and feelings. I am open to learning the lessons life has been teaching me.

I am comfortable in my own skin, and I own my power today. I am not perfect, but I am excellent.

I use to hate being by myself, but today, as my own best friend, I have learned to enjoy my own company. Today I enjoy it so much, I can sometimes find myself isolating.

Balance in everything.
I am joy.
I am peace.
I am a child of God.

I am.

TEACHER MOVIES

The Blackboard Jungle (1955)
The Miracle Worker (1962)
To Sir with Love (1967)
Up the Down Staircase (1967)
Goodbye Mr. Chips (1969)
The Paper Chase (1973)
Conrack (1974)

Fame (1980)
The Karate Kid (1984)
Teachers (1984)
Children of a Lesser God (1986)
Summer School (1987)
Stand and Deliver (1988)
Lean on Me (1989)
Dead Poets Society (1989)

Kindergarten Cop (1990)
Mr. Holland's Opus (1995)
Dangerous Minds (1995)
The Substitute (1996)
One Eight Seven (1997)
Good Will Hunting (1997)

Election (1999)
Sister Act (1999)
October Sky (1999)
Music of the Heart (1999)

Finding Forrester (2000)
Pay It Forward (2000)
Remember the Titans (2000)
The Emperor's Club (2002)
Mona Lisa Smile (2003)
School of Rock (2003)
Sky High (2005)
Coach Carter (2005)

Half Nelson (2006)
The Ron Clark Story (2006)
Chalk (2006)
History Boys (2006)
The Great Debaters (2007)
Freedom Writers (2007)
Front of the Class (2008)
Precious (2009)

Detachment (2011)
Beyond the Blackboard (2011)
The Hunt (2012)
McFarland (2015)
The Man Who Knew Infinity (2015)
The Teacher (2016)

CHAPTER 3

Life as a Substitute Teacher

SUB TEACHER ROLL CALL
HIGH SCHOOL IN SCARSDALE
N.Y.

Harper	Brooks	Serena
Wilder	Addison	Channing
Ainsley	Clay	Audrey
Buckley	Reed	Niles
Aidan	Courtney	Kerri
Saxon	Scarlett	Leighton
Amelie	Blaine	Bunny
Royce	Taylor	Cole
Sterling	Ingram	Ellison
Pierce	Blair	Hugh
Blythe	Thompson	Buffy

Prank Names #1

Adam Bomb

Barbie Dahl

Carrie Oakey

Fran Tick

Hammond Eggs

Igor Beever

Juan Manband

Lee King

Mark Z. Spot

IS GEEST HERE?

The first day of school from elementary through secondary school, including every semester of college and graduate school, when taking attendance the teacher or professor would often say,

"Is James here? James GEEST?

*"No, my last name is pronounced Geist,
with the long I (eye)
as in Poltergeist"*

In my German class in 8th grade
Frau Sandt taught us:

"ei" sounds like "i" and
"ie" sounds like "e."

I am half German,
and received a D in
German class.

Frau Sandt may have given me
a "D" in middle school,
but she knew how to
pronounce my
last name.

DAY ONE AS A SUBSTITUTE TEACHER IN N.Y.C.

It is 1998, and I am now a substitute teacher in New York City. I am transitioning from full time minister to becoming a history teacher.

After filling out many forms, and getting finger printed, and having a criminal background check, and passing the interview, I am now teaching at a Middle School in Astoria Queens.

Day One: It is period one and my room is in a long hallway, no security agents to be found. I am in a room full of rowdy kids and it is chaos. I do not believe the teacher left any work for the students that day. Usually it does not matter – when the teacher is out, whether there is student work or not, the kids usually treat it as a free period.

I finish taking roll call, and a young man runs in room, and begins pummeling a girl. They have not given me a phone list, so I tell a student to run to the Principal's Office. I run to the fight. The girl is on the floor, and the boy is punching her. I grab him by the scruff off his neck and arm, and pull him off the girl who is hyper-ventilating.

Another girl runs out of the room and says, "You touched him! I am reporting you!" Security finally shows up with an A.P. I report what happened. I save a girl from really getting injured. Yea me!

At the end of period 8, on the loud speaker is an announcement for Mr. Geist to report to the Principal's Office. I am let go, despite helping a girl from getting injured. *I guess I should have let the aggressor pummel the young lady until security showed up.*

SUBSTITUTE TEACHER TRAINING (circa 2016)

The two hour summer training stresses,
"This is not baby sitting.
We want you to engage *our* students!"
My first day at Warwick High School
was the Tuesday after Columbus Day and
we debate if Columbus Day should be a Federal
holiday.

President Franklin D. Roosevelt pushed for the
holiday before his next election to gain the vote of
the recently emigrated Italians to the States.

I share of the rape, pillaging and genocide
committed by Columbus' men
on their second voyage back to the New World.

I see a young person in the back of the room
giving me the stink eye.

Hey kid, don't kill the messenger,
the Human Resources Department
for the Warwick NY Education Department
said to engage, not babysit.

The next day I report to the High School
and I am told my services are no longer needed.
I ask for an explanation, but none is given.

I have taught classes of mostly Dominicans, classes
half Dominican and half African American in NYC,
and they never cell phone called their parents to
snitch to the Principal.

These Anglo children have got rights,
all this anti-bullying campaigning
has made them oversensitive
to the reality of the history
of human cruelty to other human beings.

As a sub,
I am at the bottom
of the educational food chain:
no meeting,
no explanation,
no warning
no second chances
at THIS school.

Sometimes yes means no.
Sometimes no is really a yes.
I bought into the PR presentation
for the "sake of the children."

From now on, I will nod my head
when the trainers say "Engage!,"
but in reality,
I will take attendance,
hand out the work,
and baby-sit
to collect my bi-monthly check.

I'as got bills and a mortgage to pay.

EARLY SCHEDULE
June 2018 West Milford High School

I am called in for a substitute teaching assignment for the school's German teacher who is named Ms. Early.

I report to the school office and Mary Ann the executive school secretary calls my name. She pulls out a small orange sheet of paper, writes out 1 through 8 and begins putting room numbers next to each number plus my lunch period.

There are several types of schedules the school follows when not on a "regular schedule." There is a delayed opening, early dismissal, double first, double second, double third and pep rally.

The secretary says, "You are the German teacher today - you are on the Early schedule."

    I say, "We are on an early schedule today?"

Mary Ann says, "Who said we are on an early schedule? Where did you get that idea?"

I say, "I could have sworn you said we are on the early schedule."

She asks the other secretary, "Are we on the early schedule today?" The other secretary says, "No, it is a regular schedule today."

The subbing secretary does not suffer fools well, so I choose to keep quiet. I can choose to be right and keep my peace.

She double checks my schedule and says, "Okay, here is the schedule for the German teacher, Ms. Early."

I say, "That is why I thought you said we were on an "Early Schedule" today. When you first called me, you told me, you are on the Early schedule."

She shakes her head and smiles.

See, I was on the Early schedule (the teacher), not the "early schedule" when classes are shortened and the kids are dismissed at 12:19.

Who is on first base?

THE RESENTFUL SUB

He taught Math in Florida for 20 years and then moved to New Jersey and taught for another decade. He was now retired but came in
for substitute teaching three days a week.

As he sat across from me in the lunch room
taking the sandwich out of his brown bag and
I asked him "How are you doing?'

>With a sour puss face he responded, "Shitty."
>He was irritated, angry, sad and disgusted.

"How can I not be doing shitty, after spending all of my life teaching, I have to still work as a sub to make ends meet? I was paid so little, I have to work in my retirement years."

I am 53 years old, working as the monitor of a Suspension Room, trying to land a full time job as a Social Studies Teacher.

The disgruntled sub says, *"Listen pal, when you hit 50 years old, your career is over. No one is hiring 50 or over."* He gets up to leave the room to use the bathroom.

I say to the other teacher in the room, "I find his blunt sharing to be refreshing." The other teacher nods his head in agreement.

UNISEX BATHROOMS

I work at a school in Newark that has unisex bathrooms. They consist of one stall and a sink for cleaning up. It is the republic of relieving oneself – truly the most democratic.

I am subbing in West Milford New Jersey and I feel the call of nature. I have to wiz like a White Rhino. I also have to be at my next class in three minutes.

There is someone in the male faculty bathroom, and the female faculty bathroom is open. What to do? I could use the male bathroom on the other side of the building, or on the 2nd floor, but those could be occupied as well. I really have to go.

I make an executive decision and I go in the female faculty bathroom and lock the door. I make sure I put the toilet seat up when I am done, and I walk out to she teacher giving me the stink eye.

She gives me the "How dare you!" look. It is as if I have passed wind in front of the Queen Mother. The offended female teacher says, "WRONG BATHROOM!"

If I saw a woman walk out of the men's room, I would think, *Good for her!* I wonder if "Mrs. Pissy" has separate bathrooms in her home: perhaps one for male, female and transgender. So territorial some people – sheesh.
    Where are the equal rights?
    Where is the equal energy?

The Committed Teacher

The High School teacher, aged 72, confided in me,
"I will be working until I am 76."

"Wow, you must really be committed to your craft!"

The septuagenarian pedagogue replied,
"I emigrated to this country late in my life.
I must work until age 76 to get my
Social Security 40 quarters (10 years) to
be eligible for Social Security and Medicare.

His commitment was to
getting healthcare and
retirement income was
equal to investing in
the future of teens.

I identify!

When I turn 65,
I plan on collecting
Social Security and
Medicare.
50% of the people I know
who have died,
before age 65!

Being a pensioner is not
for wussies or those who
are not able to live past age 65.

SCHOOL
1950's vs. the 2010's

1950's

Dad shares a story of his elementary school days. During lunch break, one of the students found a praying mantis.

Students gathered around to look at it. One student said, "I am going to step on it and kill the bug!"

Someone else says, "You can't do that. It is against the law to kill a praying mantis!"

The other kids nod in agreement and the praying mantis lives.

2010's

During lunch break at an elementary school, a student finds a praying mantis.

Students gather around to look at the green freakish monster of an insect.

Someone says, "I am going to step on the bug!" Someone else says, "No you are not!"

"You cannot step on it, unless we all can join in on the stomping! Who cares about the law?"

Respect is never old fashioned.

THE RESENTFUL SUB

He taught Math in Florida for 20 years and then moved to New Jersey and taught for another decade. He was now retired but came in
for substitute teaching three days a week.

As he sat across from me in the lunch room
taking the sandwich out of his brown bag and
I asked him "How are you doing?"

>With a sour puss face he responded, "Shitty."
>He was irritated, angry, sad and disgusted.

"How can I not be doing shitty, after spending all of my life teaching, I have to still work as a sub to make ends meet? I was paid so little, I have to work in my retirement years."

I am 53 years old, working as the monitor of a Suspension Room, trying to land a full time job as a Social Studies Teacher.

The disgruntled sub says, *"Listen pal, when you hit 50 years old, your career is over. No one is hiring 50 or over."* He gets up to leave the room to use the bathroom.

I say to the other teacher in the room, "I find his blunt sharing to be refreshing." The other teacher nods his head in agreement.

PRISON GUARD TEACHER

As a substitute teacher, I work with teacher aides
who help with the Special Education classes.
When that is the case, I generally let the aides run
the class, and I act as the class aide's aide.

The teaching assistant is a big girl,
blond hair, blue eyes
and an even bigger attitude than her girth.
She is unfriendly, curt and seems quite unhappy.
I say "Hello" to her in the hallways,
and she walks past me as if I am invisible.

During the Social Studies class on World War II,
I share a few facts with them.
The students break into pairs and work
when Ms. Aide, with squinted eyes,
goose stepping towards me
gives me a dressing down making it clear,
I should remain silent.
she says "I have everything under control."
I think, *"Ya volt! I know nothing!"*

I imagine this aide as one of
the 3,700 hundred female guards
who worked for the Nazis.
I imagine her giving roll call,
with heavy boots, whip and pistol.

I can imagine her flogging prisoners
and shooting people randomly,
enjoying the fear it created among
the female concentration camp prisoners.
I can see her releasing the half-starved dogs
savaging the female prisoners.

I stop myself from thinking such things
when she tells the class,
"My Grandfather grew up in Germany
and was child when Hitler became the leader.
He remembers how bad the economy was
and the many hungry nights he suffered as a boy.
Hitler promised a chicken in every pot,
and Hitler fulfilled his promise."

This teacher's assistant even looks like
the Auschwitz guard Irma Grese,
one of Joseph Mengele's lovers.
Irma Grese was known as "the Beautiful Beast,"
and on December 13th, 1945,
was led to the gallows
and executed by long-drop hanging
for her role in the Final Solution.

The "Hyena of Auschwitz"
went from a teen milk maid to volunteer murderer.
Irma Grese left school at age 14
with poor scholastic aptitude
 and was bullied by classmates.

Hysterical means historical
I wonder what childhood hurts
have given the teacher's aide
such a mean exterior?

Who bullied you Herr Aide?
I pray you get the healing you deserve.

How do we get world peace?
Heal your inner child.

BLAST FROM THE PAST
May 21, 2018

I just finished teaching a nice gig in Maplewood/South Orange at Columbia High School in New Jersey. It is a well to do area where parents are doctors, lawyers, and work for corporations in NYC and many are avid MsNBC watchers. The parents also value education.

My long term teaching fill in job finishes. I am sad, I have filled the room with $200 full of posters, and I will miss the students. The Principal and Assistant Principal are very happy with my service and would be open to hiring me should a position open up in the near future.

I am back to subbing at West Milford Junior High School second period. As I stand in the hallway welcoming students, a young lady walks up to me, smiles and says "Hello!" Very nice I think.

Twenty minutes into the student work the young lady says, "Mr. Geist, did you use to teach at Merit Prep Charter School in Newark?" I say, "Yes." She says, "My name is Quinn and I had you for class."

I pull up a desk next to her, and we talk. I remember Quinn being a good student and well behaved. She says, "Mr. Geist, our class was terrible to you."

WAS THE CLASS OF URBAN STUDENTS TERRIBLE TO ME?

I was the dead floating whale carcass, and the students were the Great White sharks taking bites out of me.

I was the fish carcass eaten to the bone by the Amazonian piranhas.

I was the Zebra taken down by a Nile Crocodiles at the shallow crossing.

I was the gazelle devoured by the pack of laughing hyenas.

I was the missionary of the mid-1800's eaten by cannibals and have my head shrunk.

Quin's father moved her from Newark to West Milford to help his daughter get a better education. Turns out, they moved just seven houses down the street from my home on the same street.

    I shall invite them over for a campfire.

PRINCIPLE or PRINCIPAL?

A principle is a
general or
fundamental law;
a rule or code of conduct.

I use to work for
Principal Frank Brancato
who use to say,

"My title is spelled
P-R-I-N-C-I-P-A-L.
You can always remember
the spelling because the
Principal is your "pal."

Some students and
some teachers
did not agree;
but
he and I
got along.

Chapter 4

The Life of a Teacher

SUB TEACHER ROLL CALL
HIGH SCHOOL IN WASHINGTON HEIGHTS N.Y.C.

Sofia	Pablo	Josephina
Mateo	Emily	Pedro
Isabella	Ignacio	Isadora
Leonardo	Guadalupe	Miguel
Martina	Emilio	Alessandra
Angel	Emily	Jorge
Lucia	Christian	Alexa
Maximo	Bianca	Esteban
Maria	Javier	Manuela
Ivan	Jazmin	Jesus
Catalina	Manuel	Renata
Luis	Mia	Eduardo

Prank Names #2

Al E. Gator

Bea Sting

Chris Mass

Dan Druff

Frank Furter

Harry Butz

Ima Hogg

Justyn Tyme

Lou Natic

Mary Wana

YES SIR MADAME TEACHER
(circa 1975)

Mrs. Becker was my music teacher
at Union Terrace Elementary
in fourth grade aged 9.
The boys use to argue
"If you had to marry the
Music, Art or Gym teacher,
which one?" I always chose
Ms. Gatos the art teacher,
others Ms. Carol.

I had just seen a military movie
over the weekend and the soldiers
kept saying "Yes Sir!" or "No Sir!"

In music class I am in the back row
Fooling around and not paying attention
And we are singing
John Jacob Jingle Heimer Schmidt
or Swing Low Sweet Chariots or
Jimmy Crack Corn when -

Mrs. Becker calls my name.
Thinking I am showing respect,
I say "Yes Sir!"
She gets up from her synthesizer seat,
briskly walks over to the back row
and picks me up by the back curlies
of my reddish hair.

"WHAT DID YOU SAY?"
"Yes Sir?"
"I AM TO BE CALLED MAM!"
I learned something that day.

SCHOOL AUTHORITY
U.S. vs. the PHILIPPINES

Before the 1980's, teachers were monarchs of the classroom. Teachers could grab a kid, take him in the hallway, rough him up, and if the school called home, the student received a second whooping at home as well.

It changed when cell phones were allowed in schools. Students could stir up things for a teacher, then turn on the phone to record the teacher losing it.
In 2016, yelling a student can be considered "corporal punishment."

In the Philippines, teachers can do the following with students:
strike, pinch
pull hair,
smack a head against the board, and/or make them stand in the hot sun in the courtyard for an hour. If you do not have a pen or your notebook, you are sent home to fetch it.

I do not support using any of the above for giving a wrong answer as some Filipino teachers do, but for classroom management purposes, having discipline privileges maximize the most time possible for education.

In Tagalag, "oh-oh," means yes. I say "oh-oh" to the "ouch-ouch" of using a yard stick on the students who are disrespectful and joking around too much.

Consequences make a difference for efficient classroom management.

PROFESSIONAL PEDAGOGICAL SERVICE
Fall 2011-Spring 2012

Marking Periods taught: 6 marking periods

Days of teaching: 170

Hours of teaching: 707 hours

Instruction Interruptions: 4, 250

***Satisfactory Ratings: 12 in a row

Classes: 850 classes

Lessons prepared: 340 lessons

Students taught: 125 over 2 semesters

Weekly Attendance Sheets: 36 weeks of classes

Parental Phone Calls: 150

Tests administered: 60

Substitute Lesson Plans created: 9-10

Emergency Teacher Coverage's: 6

Regent Exams administered: 2 U.S. Regents
 (2 summer exams)   2 Regent Exams

Class Grades turned in: 12

Total Grades tallied: 1,500

HW assigned: 360

Parent Teacher Conferences: 3 out of 4 days

Bulletin Boards; Hallway: 1   Classroom: 4

Word Walls: 72

Copies made: 1700

Assemblies attended: 4

Fights broken up: 1 x a semester = 2

Belittling comments by students: 850

Chalk Boards Cleaned: 340

Desks Cleaned: 3,240

Faculty Meetings: 9

Departmental meetings: 9

Professional Development Meetings: 3-4

Attempted Poisoning?:
 -cleaning fluid poured into my drinking bottle.

Days Commuting to Work: 13,940 miles.

AWARD: TEACHER OF THE YEAR: 1 x

Smoke Breaks and Candy Crush

In 2018,
research showed
that workers who take smoke breaks
during work waste 6 days
of productivity
a year.

Research also shows.
workers lose 8 hours a week
of productivity by playing
on their cell phones
equaling 10 days
of productivity
a year.

Non-smokers
are asking
for an extra six days of
vacation per year.

I should get
an extra 16 days
of vacation since
I neither smoke
nor own
a cell phone.

Gumby & Mr. Roboto
Circa 1990

My former college dorm neighbor becomes a teacher in Vermont. His name was Peter, we called him "Gumby," and his students called him Mr. W. Gumby is creative, humorous history teacher with his smart aleck Long Island attitude and love for God and the heart of a servant.

On this Spring day he teaches a lesson about robots on the playground and asks for a volunteer that he wraps in aluminum foil and masking tape while playing the song "Mr. Roboto" by the rock group Styx.

Sammy volunteers and happens to suffer from albinism. Sammy walks around in a robotic suit of aluminum foil on this hot day, reflecting off his robotic suit, as Mr. W. teaches his lesson to the background music of "Mr. Roboto."

Frantically, Sammy in a non-robotic voice screams, "Mr. W, Mr. W, I am burning up! Help!. Help! I am on fire!" The kid who was whiter than white, was cooking faster than the song "Hot, Hot, Hot!" by Buster Poindexter. Several kids jumped in ripping the aluminum foil off Sammy like a Christmas gift whose body looked like a New Year's Day Ham.

When turning a human into a robot on a warm sunny day, it is best to avoid using students surviving from albinism.

Teacher's Lunch Room
West Milford High School
November 2018

Blah, blah, blah...
Does anyone watch the
Naked and Afraid TV Show?

Yea – blah, blah, blah.

Imagine trying
to survive 21 days
in the jungle naked
with all those wild
animals and insects.

I chime in,

Working in a
public school is
like being on the show
Naked and Afraid,
but
without the
naked part.

The teachers laugh
and nod in agreement as they
chew, chomp on their dinner
leftovers of meatloaf, pizza and
baked chicken legs the day
before the Thanksgiving break.

Confession 62

Fire Drills

As a teacher
when I had
no students
in class,
I hid
in my room
at least
4-5 times
during the
monthly
fire drill;

I was
working
on
school work
or
the weather
was
cold
or
inclement.

Sinus Headache
January 2020

3 am:	splitting sinus headache
3:01 am:	a few curse words
3:04 am:	Sudafed – watch Forensic Files on TV
3:20 am:	left side of head beginning to clear
3:21 am:	Vicks Vapor Rub on chest and nostrils
4:29 am:	take "breathe-easy" strip off the nose
4:30 am:	hot shower
4:35 am:	left side of head 90% cleared
4:40 am:	cough drops
5 am:	right side of head still hurting
5:30 am:	leave for work on this 16 degree day
5:45 am	take two Excedrin pills
6 am:	most of congestion gone
6:45 am:	Ahhhhhh - RELIEF!
6:46 am:	Amen, Hallelujah!

Confession 65
Student Fight

As a
student fight
broke out
in the hallway
between
periods 3-4,
a petite
English teacher
with blond hair
hit me in the arm
and screeched,
"Get in there!
Break it up!"

I looked
at her and
wanted to say,

Sister,
in the age of
equal rights,
be my guest.
Step into the middle
of the crazed
student frenzy
and earn your
equal pay!

RETIREMENT DAY
(Summer of 2017)

It is mid-June and there is no more need for subs.

My budget is tight, but I am okay because
I have summer school to teach
and a friends house to paint.

Summer school is canceled,
and so is the friend's will to
have the house painted.

I get on the horn and call 50 painting contractors.
I get a summer painting for Rulhio's Painting.

Paul says, **"I know the exact day I am retiring."**
I am on the 28 foot ladder taping windows
for Dominican Popo, the spray painter,
and next to me on the 36 footer is Paul.

Paul use to be a chef, but the chef salary
promised never came to fruition,
He grew tired of the corporate world
and the kitchen politics
and started house painting
with his hermano.

Paul bought his home just
before the housing bubble burst
and paying $200,000 more
than the house if valued today.

I hope to still get my
own home painting job.
I hear on the next job,
we are working on 60 foot ladders
and a slate roof with high pitch.
My legs get shaky after 40 feet.

I prefer being my own boss.
The money is better and
Sometimes I can cut out
early from the job.

I ask, **"So Paul, what day will you retire?**

"On the day I die,
is my
retirement
day."

BED BUGS (2016)

My wife wakes up with a bug bite on her left hand. It goes from looking like a mosquito bite to a warm angry red swelling over a three day period. The bite becomes a crusty oozing scab for two days, and then takes another 3-4 days to heal up.

I get bitten on my left forearm a few days later. I have never seen a bite like this before; it is a grotesque thing to gaze upon. Over a five week period, we are both bitten almost every week on various parts of the body.

There has been an outbreak of bed bugs at the Newark school I work at, and I suspect I have brought into my home via the canvas satchel I carry to and from school every day.

We never locate the suspect. One Saturday, I see a bug exterminator at my neighbors and explain my dilemma, but he is no help. He wants to get out of dodge to go fishing. I figured by the description of the bite, he would have an idea of the culprit.

It is not a mosquito and we can find no spiders in the room. I sometimes get cave crickets in the summer in the downstairs workroom, and perhaps one snuck upstairs. They look like prehistoric bugs with their camouflage coloring jumping at humans with cocky brazen bravado that would make martial arts expert Claude Van Dam jump like a kangaroo.

I am bitten again just above my right eye, and by Wednesday, my eye is almost closed, and I have the privilege of immature 6th graders staring at me and making smart ass comments all day.

The wife and I go to Allentown for the weekend, and I open a can of some insect bomb Saturday morning before we leave. The poison spays out the top like the water mist of a vaporizer with Vicks menthol flavoring.

We return Sunday, open windows to air out the room. The bomb kills the unknown bug, and we can sleep without fear again.

PULL OVER PLEASE

In my northern New Jersey
town of 27,000 the
down town center is
a triangle of three streets,
a 5 to 6 mile drive.

Every time I drive through
town, I pass 2-3 police cars
often having one tailing me
and those sneakily hidden
to ticket speeders,
many already paying
property taxes to pay
our small town cops
and their $100,000 a year
tax funded salaries
while the cops
in Paterson average
$78,000 a year.
How can that be?

My small town
feels like a police
state to me.

Black lives matter.
LBGT lives matter.
Blue lives matter.
Do working class
commuter lives matter?

Why are the cop-pers
harassing the working class
trying to pay their monthly
mortgage,
bills,
insurance,
and
taxes to pay?

Let the workers focus
on getting to and from
their livelihoods
without fear of
getting ticketed.

I want my police force
focusing their time
and energy capturing
murderers,
rapists,
drug dealers,
burglars,
drunk drivers,
and
cold cases.

TEACHER SUMMER HOUSE PAINTING

Climb the 28 foot ladder
to paint soffits
below the gutters.

Scrape, scrape, scrape.
Spackle, spackle, spackle.
Sand, sand, sand.
Brush, brush, brush the primer.
Move ladder and repeat.

Working with an
entertaining crew of salts
in A.A., N.A.
or active in their addictions.

Hornet's nest,
fly down the ladder,
climb back up
with the wasp spray.
No stings today.

Once between the eyes,
my head swelled like a melon
and my eyes turned Asian.

Climb ladder.
Scrape.
Spackle.
Sanding.
Priming.
Move ladder.

Change the radio station.
Wash out the brush
using the garden hose
and wire brush.

First coat of finish.
Move ladder.

Coffee break.

Second coat of finish.
Move to the
other side of house
and repeat.

LUNCH;
actually
watch
paint
dry
on
walls.

Sun in eyes,
sweat in eyes,
paint droplets
in eyes and ears.

Left knee
sometimes aches,
some get tennis elbow,
is there a painter's
elbow syndrome?

I scratch an itch
on my face accidently
giving myself
a make out bandit
paint mustache.

Feeling tired from
physical labor,
heat and humidity,
I drink another coffee
and turn up the radio
and find the strength
to make it to 4:30pm.

Wax on, wax off.
paint up, paint down.
According to the
Karate Kid movie
and Mr. Miyagi,
I should have
been a martial arts
expert a decade ago.
It must feel powerful
to know you can kill a
man with your hands.

Paint chips in
my socks, shoes
underwear and hair.
At least a root canal only
lasts for an hour.

THE DISTRACTED DRIVER
5/25/21 6:35 a.m.

At the stoplight on the morning commute, in Jersey City, I look in the rearview mirror, and watch a young woman (aged 22?) playing with her long dark hair. Right hand stroke, left hand stroke, right hand stroke, left hand stroke, right hand stroke and then a head shaking her long black raven hair like she is in a shampoo commercial.

Can she see me watching her? Is she doing this for me, or for her?

Sitting in her white Kia, with a pink pine tree air freshener, and angel wings having from her rear mirror (?), the light turns green, and she is now talking on her cell phone as she drives and continues stroking her hair.

We pass Dunking Donuts on Palisades Blvd on the passenger side, and one block north of it, she makes a left hand turn into the Jersey City Hospital Parking lot.

A nurse? A person who helps other people, an angel to those in pain and/or crisis.

All is forgiven.

Special School Days

Winnie-the-Pooh asked, "Which is better? The taste of honey or the anticipation of honey?" That is how I have always felt about the last day of school before any holiday break.

1a) Columbus Day 3 day weekend aka
1b) Indigenous People's Day
2) Thanksgiving Break
3) Christmas Winter Break
4) MLK 3 day weekend
5) Presidents Day 3 day Weekend
6) Birthday
7) Spring Break
8) Memorial Day 3 day weekend
9) Last Day of School

K-12: $9 \times 13 = 117$ special days
College: $9 \times 4 = 36$ special days
Grad School: $9 \times 3 = 24$ special days
<u>Teacher $9 \times 30 = 270$ special days</u>
TOTAL   447 special days

or 1 year and 88 special days

If the S.N.L.'s Dana Carvey "Church Lady" asked me, "Isn't that special?" I'd answer, "Yes, 21 squared + 6."

TEACHER PARKING LOT AFTER SNOWSTORM
2/28/22

It snowed February 24th into February 25th. I spent an two hours on Saturday between snow blower and shovel cleaning up the driveway, back deck and front entryway to the home.

On Monday morning, as I drove to work, I knew the upper teacher parking lot, which will comfortably park 30 vehicles tightly on a nice day, could get competitive as ploughed snow piles would steal some spots, until taken care of by the giant solar shovel in the sky.

The building where I work holds two high schools in it. I am the new teacher at this school, so I do not know everyone yet, and I really don't want to cause any waves. My motto is to live under the boss radar.

I park in a spot that can comfortably allow for three cars to park. I usually pull into the lot at 7am, and sometimes take a 15-30 minute nap before entering the building. I must sign in by 8 a.m. As I am napping, I can hear someone parking next to me. It is a gray Ford Explorer, and instead of parking in a civil manner, he pulls in taking up two spots.

This really "irks" me - as a fellow teacher, where is your sense of union solidarity, or plain old civility for that matter?

I take down his license plate, and inform security. At lunch, I look out a 2nd floor window, to see he has moved his Explorer, and there are three vehicles in the 3 vehicle parking area. How difficult was that?

The next day as I am napping, the Explorer pulls next to me. The SUV horn beeps. I keep sleeping. Ten seconds later, it beeps again. I keep napping. Thirty seconds later, it beeps again. Out of the corner of my eye, the Explorer driver is at the top of the parking lot hill, pointing his keychain fob at his truck, with an annoyed look on his face.

???

I think this guy is upset he was not able to hog two parking spots.

The following day, I get in the lot before Ford Explorer guy. He parks his vehicle, and begins walking up the hill to his school entry. I get out of my C-Max and ask him, "Is there a problem?"
    What?
"Do you have a problem with me? I just want to know why you felt the need to keep hitting your car horn yesterday?"
    I have no problem Mister. What is your name?
"What is your name?"

Long story short – I pulled out the "you're a teacher, I'm a teacher card. I don't want any problems with anyone – so I just want to have a clean slate with you. We all have to work. It is all about the children."

"Bob" told me, "No problems."

This guy was too chicken s__t to tell me he was upset at me for going to security.

We now wave to each other.

We will even become friends in the future.

CAR ACCIDENT REPORT

James C. Geist
Insurance PANJ007 2016 Ford C-Max
March 10, 2022 (7:15am accident)

March 10th approximately 7 :15am on the Bayview Bridge [between Route 78 near the Liberty Center & Garfield Ave in Jersey City NJ)

Road conditions: icy, foggy, cold (33 degrees)

I knew the road conditions were icy, because I dove by 6 different car accidents on Route 78 on a mile and a half section of Route 78 West)1.5 miles before the Bayview Bridge exit. There were state police and ambulances and slow moving traffic to the exit.

I exited route78 West and began my drive to Innovation High School (I teach history) .

There are two lanes on the Bayview Bridge (between 78 and Garfield Ave Jersey City), I was in the passing lane driving approximately 25mph, and in the middle of the bridge was an SUV stopped, with no hazard lights on.

I had my seatbelt on, no passengers.   I am not award of any injuries at this time.

I put my brakes on, the C-Max slid, I pumped my brakes and began turning into the slow lane when a vehicle hit me from behind (driven by Orlando) and pushed me into the Jeep I sideswiped (Merlito – older gentleman).

Merlito and Orlando were civil and I said, "You all saw the woman parked in the middle of the bridge?" They both

Smells Like A__!

The high school kids in Jersey City will tell you what they really think. "That smells like ass" is one of them.

On Monday morning, as I walk into my classroom and take out my folders, lessons, classwork, and laptop computer to start my day, I smell something – AND it smells like "a__."

MY teacher chair! I am horrified.

I am 55, middle-aged, and my self-confidence drops to 0 in a heart beat. Why does my chair stink?

Is it me? I shower 1-2 times a day! How does this happen.

I break out the Lysol Spray, which you can find everywhere in a public school in age of Covid and spray down my chair.

It is not until lunch time, as I am chewing on a piece of pickle from my chicken salad lunch with ranch dressing and a Sherlock Holmes moment hits me, *we had state testing all week in my room, and a substitute teacher, with a big butt, sat in my chair all week!*

Voila! It takes three days of spraying my teacher chair twice a day with Lysol, and the chair finally airs itself of the "ass" smell, and my self-confidence is back to a 97!

Oh the humanity.

said yes. Merlito said to me, "I know you had to move over to avoid a collision with the womans vehicle (a dark SUV)." We all apologized to each other – recognizing it was an accident (& why we have car insurance).

My back bumper is dented and the back hatch door has scrapes. The passenger side back wheel well also is scraped up.

As the three men exchanged information with each other, the woman parked in the middle of the bridge, drove away. We did not get her information.

This is my testimony
James C. Geist
3/10/22   8:35 am
Innovation High School   Room 3

Tired

Damn am I tired!

No rest for the cherry; I mean
no rest for the cheery; I mean
no rest for the leery.
   Damn am I tired!

No rest for the query; I mean
no rest for the smeary; I mean
no rest for the Kashmiri.
   Damn am I tired!

No rest for the thirty; I mean
no rest for the dreary; I mean
no rest for the teary.
   Damn am I tired!

No rest for THE WEARY!

   TIRED!
      TiReD!
         TireD!
            Tir_____zzzzzzzzzz…

West Milford High School Parking Lot @ 3pm

Honk, honk!

VROOM, VROOM…..

Clank, clank, clank…..

Screeeeeehhhh!

Pb-pb-pb-b-b-b

Beep, Beep!

Tick, tick, tick, tick, tick…..

Rumble-rumble-rumble-sputter

VaRoom, VaRoom!

Honk, honk!

Eeeeeergh!

Pop-pop-pop-pop-pop

Vroom, vroom, VROOM!

VaRoom, Varoom_ga-ga-ga-ga-ga…..

Beep, beep!

American Healthcare is Killing Me

My first net paycheck at Mets Charter School (2019) is $2400. I work on my budget and figure out I will be able to pay my bills, take out my wife once a month for a movie and dinner, and have $500 extra left over to pay off some debt, pay some principle off the mortgage and squirrel enough away to not have to house paint or teach summer school in July or August.

My next check is $2150, $250 less or $500 less a month. They union rep tells me $500 comes out a month to pay for my health insurance.

DAMN!

This is a way NJ Governor Christie has punished teachers for being mostly Democrats by increasing teacher healthcare payments (not cops or firemen).

The American Healthcare system is killing me (financially). Single payer universal healthcare is so complicated, that only 31 of 32 first world countries are able to pull it off.

I can't believe I will spend another summer house painting to meet my monthly budge nut. When will I be able to escape ladders, scraping, sanding, priming and finish coating?

Damn!

I spit on the ground every time I hear Governor Fatty's name.

Chapter 5

The Students

SUB TEACHER ROLL CALL
HIGH SCHOOL IN CHINATOWN N.Y.C.

Zi	Xio	Bo
Feng	Jing	Quon
Mei	Ning	Huo
Dewel	Tai	Shan
Ji	Yi	Ling
Chen	Li	Jie
Yang	Zhin	Kiew
Bao	Ning	Chi
Cai	Bo	Enlai
Chang	Jia	Fai
Wei	Dishi	Xiang
Li-mei	Chai	Genji

Prank Names #3

Al Koholic

Beau Vine

Chris P. Bacon

Dick Tater

Cary Oakie

Helen Back

Jacques Strappe

Lou Sirr

Miya Buttreeks

SCHOOL LUNCH LOTTO
(circa 1980)

I am liked by the
lunch lady in
Middle School.
Somehow I end
up with extra
scoops of

mashed potatoes,
chicken nuggets,
fries,
Salisbury steak,
meatballs,
chicken legs or
dessert.

I am cute,
I am likeable;

but other students
get wise to the
favoritism

and ask the lunch lady
why James gets
special treatment –

but that is how it is
when the lunch lady is
your Aunt Arlene.

Juvenile Detention Student

It was my first year teaching
in NYC in 1999.
In the middle of the year,
A tall African American teen
walks into my class.
He shows me his schedule
and he is in my class.

Nothing unusual, the
school is a 50-50 mix of
African American and Dominican.
When I ask where he came
From he says, "Spafford."

I later ask my union representative,
"What is Spafford?"
I am informed it is
a juvenile detentions center
in the Bronx.

The next day I ask the new
student why he was sent to Spafford
and he tells me, "In my last school,
I punched my teacher in the face."

I look at him and say,
"Welcome to my classroom."
The kid sat in the back of the class
and never gave me a problem.

MY LOCA LATINA STUDENT
(circa Spring 2000)

It was my first year teaching
at Park West High School
in Hell's Kitchen NYC.

I have a Puerto Rican female,
Who is the barometer of the class.
When she acts up,
The whole class acts up –
And she has been acting up
WAY too much lately.

I have tried talking,
calling home,
writing dean referrals –
this kid is incorrigible.

I am in a foul mood this
day teaching, and soooo
tired of Ms. Latina's act.

I call her into
The hallway and say,
"I just wanted you to know Miss,
I served in the Persian Gulf War
in 1991 and have 5 confirmed kills
AND I also shot over a dozen camels
for the fun of it while I served there,"

I give her the 1,000 yard stare.

She says,
"Yo Mister,
You are crazy!"

I respond saying,
"That's right,
I am crazy,
and I have had
enough of your
UNACCEPTABLE
behavior in my class.
From that day on, she behaved.

Amazing what a teacher
has to do for
"classroom management"
to create
a classroom where
education can take place.

Many teachers,
especially in urban districts
suffer from Post Traumatic
Stress Disorder, but it is not
talked about much.

I felt some guilt about lying
since I had been a pastor
for five years - however,
being able teach in this particular
class made my lie
worth it for the kids
who wanted to learn.

"Mr. Incredible"

In 2004, the animated movie
"The Incredibles" comes out
about a family of four
who must hide their powers
to live a quiet suburban life.

The family must combine
forces to defeat a killer robot
named Syndrome.

The father figure
has strawberry blond hair,
is a big guy with a big chest
and a pot belly to match.

My students at the
High School of Health Careers
and Sciences begin calling me
"Mr. Incredible."

My defensive, dysfunctional
and punitive Assistant Principal
gets miffed when she gets wind
students call me Mr. Incredible.
She tells me it is egotistical
to call oneself Mr. Incredible.

I inform her,
"The students call me that,
I did not name myself
Mr. Incredible."

Whenever we debrief from
A classroom observation,
I end the meetings by saying,

"I am not perfect,
but I am excellent."

She hated
when I said that…

which is
why I did.

MY STUDENT OSAMA

Osama is a quiet kid

and a good student.

He keeps to himself.

The 9/11 2001 attack occurs.

I tell Osama he might consider

changing his name.

I also tell him I hope he joins

the F.B.I. to work undercover to help

us locate terrorist cell groups.

U.S. intelligence

needs people who already

Speak Middle Eastern languages.

MY N___GA!
(2,000)

I teach my first semester at Park West High School
on 50th Street between 10th and 11th Avenues.
I get a pink slip for the second semester,
the school population always drops
as the year passes.

A union brother steps down from being a Dean,
and I teach three classes and dean for two.
His act of solidarity saves my job.

I am a tough but fair dean.
I treat all the same.
Those who have never had me as a teacher,
and have only seen me in the hallways,
think I am mean.

I am really the misunderstood Boo Bradley
in To Kill A Mockingbird,
or the Monster
in Frankenstein.

I walk down the hallway
and pass two students,
one Dominican,
the other African American.

The one student says to the other,
"I hate that guy!
 He is the meanest person in our school"

The other student responds,
"Hey, don't anything bad about Mr. Geist!
Mr. Geist is my nigga!"

GIRL GRAPPLER
(circa 2001)

"You are ugly"
said the high school boy to a girl
in the NYC School hallway by room 325.
He taunted her,
gave her a push and
began to box slap her.

The young lady
gets into boxing pose and
starts prancing like Sugar Ray Leonard.

She throws a left jab to his stomach,
The boy buckling over from the blow,
and she catches him in the chin
with a right hook.

The young man goes down,
never realizing the young women
went to the gym
every day
to train as a boxer.

He transfers to another school.
bullies do not like
to be mocked
and made fun of,
especially when the bully is
whooped by a girl.

There is justice in the world sometimes.

MY CHILDREN

"Yo Mister, how many
children do you have?"

*"I have 125 children.
All my students are
my children."*

"No, no, how many
kids do you have
at home?"

"Oh, I don't have any."

"Why don't you have
any children?"

*"Well, as a teacher,
I get to observe
children's actions daily
in the classroom,
  so I chose to not
  have any children. In
fact, I had a vasectomy*

"Yo Mister, that's messed
up. That's wrong to
say."

Another student chimes out,

"No, Mr. 'G' is right,
 look at the way students
act in our school."

STIFF-ARMED

It is a rainy November morning as the 2018 Cadillac C75 V Sedan pulls up to the front entrance of the local high school in northern New Jersey.

The middle aged father with his gray hair and goatee mustache gets out of the driver's side as the daughter in black sweatpants and her yellow and black school jacket holding her notebook and school book exits from the back door.

The father stands there with his arms semi-open hoping to get a hug of affection, and the daughter turns the opposite way walking around the car trunk up the stairs not noticing him or it.

The father looks at the sky, and with sadness sits down, driving away looking sad and dejected through the driver seat side window.

It was as if Chicago Bears football running back Walter Payton had just stiff-armed Steelers linebacker Jack Lambert with his missing front teeth.

I ponder if she will buy Dad a Father's Day Card and if he will get a hug on that day.

School Day (September 10, 2021)

Conversation #1
May I go to the bathroom?
Yes. Please sign out and write the time down.
What time is it?
The wall clock is right there.
I can't read a wall clock.

Conversation #2
Can I copy your class notes?
Of course. Do you need a pencil or paper?
No. I will just take a picture of your notes with my smart phone.

Conversation #3
I don't understand your comments on my classwork.
Really? Why?
I don't read cursive writing.

S.M.H.

Do I Need to "Will Smith" You?

Classes are different, just as the energies and smells of homes are different. Some classes are quiet, come in, sit down and wait for the lesson to start.

My period 6 and period 8 classes, this 2021-22 school year, are large, are "lively" and have 5-8 "yappers" in each class. I wait for the class to settle down before starting class.

The yappers keep talking as if I am invisible. Sometimes I start showing a video on the large New Board, which are just like the video screens you see on CNN on election night continuous updates.

It is March 28th, and my patience wears thin, as I wait to start class. In a loud voice I say, "To those talking in the back of class, do I need to Will Smith you?" The class breaks out in a lively laugh. When the laughing ends, I start class. Oy.

Background

On March 27th, 2022, during a live television broadcast of the 94th Academy Awards, host Chris Rock's comedic monologue, included a joke about actor Jada Pinkett's Smith's shaved head.

Rock said, "Jada, I love you. G.I. Jane 2, can't wait to see it, alright? [audience laughs].

Actor husband Will Smith, walked up to Chris Rock and slapped him across the face. Audience members assumed it was a planned publicity stunt. It was not. Pinkett Smith has shaved her head since 2021 due to alopecia areata.

HER TALKING MADE ME AN ATHEIST
(circa 2,000 @ GWHS in NYC)

The State wants higher test scores,
the City wants higher test scores,
the Principal wants higher test scores,
I wanted higher test scores,
yet Yesenia would not stop talking in class.

In the Global History Regents class,
I have soooo much curriculum to cover;
focusing on topics that re-occur yearly on the state test,
yet Yesenia would not stop talking in class.

As Yesenia loved Jesus, Yesenia also did not care about distracting the friends she talked to, or the other students trying to listen, or to the fact she was distracting the teaching process for the teacher, or that she was not absorbing vital material to pass the test she had to pass to graduate. Yesenia did not care about what NY State, or NYC, or the Principal and the Department chair wanted. Yesenia cared about talking, talking, talking.

Yesenia, you have convinced me there is no God."
She gave me a puzzled-offended look.
I pray and I pray and I pray every day week after week to God that you will stop talking in class......AND YOU KEEP TALKING – which proves there is no God.

Twenty years later she tells me it was one of her "epic memories" from High School days, and even with the "epic-ness" she kept talking. State scores will increase with the legalization of Taser gunning of the uncivilized.

The Belligerent Suspension Room Student

To the teachers he said,
"I don't care!"

To his father he said,
"I don't care!"

To the guidance counselor he said,
"I don't care!"

To the Assistant Principal he said,
"I don't care!"

To the Principal he said,
"I don't care."

To the Social Worker he said,
"I don't care!"

To the Child Study Team workers he said,
"I don't care!"

To the School Psychologist he said,
"I don't care!"

The young man was nice to me
as the suspension room coordinator.
I was lucky - he liked me.

The young man had the power
to not care because in three years
he would be buried by cancer.

The Hulk

Vincent is a student who use to stop by the Suspension room daily at the end of the school day to say hello. He was high on the autism spectrum, and with his great attitude, was going to do well in life.

He was a Special Education student who worked at McDonalds, was on the wrestling team and went to the Prom with his date.   He was a gentleman and I looked forward to our daily conversations. Vinny was a highlight of my 2018-19 school year.

On the last day of school, in a room of seven students in the "Refocusing Center," Vincent stormed in the room with the A.P. right behind him.

A mini-riot broke among some excited seniors who were graduating. Of course, the security cameras caught all of the trouble-makers.

You spit on the floor, and now you will not walk in the graduation ceremony!

Vinny grabbed a desk, lifted it up and threw it on the ground.

And now you are not allowed to attend the graduation ceremony!

Vinny grabbed another desk, picked it up and threw it on the ground.

Follow me, I now have to call the police.

All I could think was, "This kid made it through his senior year, and now at the 1 yard line and 99/100 of the way to graduation, lost some control.

At the end of the day, when cooler heads prevailed, the A.P. walked in with Vinny and said, *Vinny wants to talk with you.*

"Mr. Geist, I am embarrassed how I acted in front of you. It was inappropriate, and I don't want you remembering me this way. I want to make sure my slate with you is clean."

He leaned over and with tears in his eyes, gave me a big hug. "Please don't think less of me. I have high regard for you."

Vinny always had my respect, but even more so that he was able to admit mistakes and apologize for them.

Vinny walked graduation the next day and is a Facebook friend of mine.

SCHOOL NURSE'S BATHROOM MIRROR

There are two bathrooms
in the nurse's office in the
local high school.
In one bathroom,
there is a mirror,
in the other bathroom
there is no mirror – by
the request of some students.

Imagine teenagers so hating
the way the look, so
hating themselves, they
they cannot stand to look at
themselves in a mirror?

In the mirror in the second bathroom
is a sticker on the lower left-hand corner
that says, "You are beautiful.
Thanks for existing,"
Love, The Universe.

In both bathrooms are signs that
say, "Please wash your hands."
Both bathrooms also have a signs
that say, "Please put down
the toilet seat when
you are finished."

Here is not looking at you kid.

Mom's Advice to her Black Son

Don't put your hands in your pocket.
Don't put your hoodie on.
Don't be outside without a shirt on.
Check in with your people, even if your down the street.
Don't be out late.
Don't touch anything you are not buying.
Never leave the store without a bag & receipt, even for
	gum.
Never make it look like there is an altercation with another.
Never leave the house without I.D.
Don't go in public with a wife-beater or du-rag.
Don't ride with music too loud.
Don't stare at a white woman.
If a cop pulls you over, and starts questioning,
	-don't talk back.
If you ever get pulled over by a cop, put your hands on the
	dashboard, and ask if you can get your license and
	registration.

-Cameron Welch via tiktok.com
*18 year old black boy

"I got, "Look both ways before crossing a street." My mother never taught me "Always get a receipt. This is white privilege."   -M. Hans Liebert@mhansliebert

"I am a white parent and the only thing I have in common with Cameron's Mom's rules is we told our kids is "don't be out late." I did not have those rules because of white privilege. Black Lives Matter!"

-Vance Vaillancourt@coach014

FUTURE TEACHERS OF AMERICA

At the beginning of the school year, I asked all my students what they wanted to do for a living. I had three smart young ladies who all said "Teachers!"

At the end of the semester, I asked the students again, what they wanted to do for a living when they finished college, and everyone gave the same answers, until I got to the three smart young ladies.

This time they answered "Nurses!" I asked them why they changed their minds from teaching to nursing they said, "After sitting in your class, we realized how disrespectful many of your students are.

Did I mention these young ladies were smart?

CLASS ROOM PEACEFULNESS

There is nothing better than when a
room full of students gets engaged
in a project or assignment and the
room becomes silent….unless
someone lets out a loud fart
in the middle of the silence.

You can forget the next 10 minutes;
students will be laughing
giggling and
making farting sounds…

…to mimic
what happened earlier
in class.

Sometimes all you
can do is laugh.

EDUCATIONAL EXCUSES

Malcolm X devoured books on history, philosophy and religion while he did his time in prison. "Reading opened new vistas to me. Reading changed the course of my life."

Rev. Dr. Martin Luther King said, " The function of education is to teach one to think intensively and critically. Intelligence plus character is the true goal of true education."

It always bothered me when my students of color would say to the African American students who excelled academically, "Stop acting white!"

What would these leaders in the African American community say about the pursuit of education? Is ethnicity an excuse for mediocrity?

Rosa Parks	**Muhammad Ali**
John Lewis	**Malcolm X**
Dr. Angela Davis	**Rev. Martin Luther King**
Stokely Carmichael	**Julian Bond**
Edward George Alcorn:	physicist, inventor
Augusta Alice Ball:	chemist
Emmett Chappelle:	scientist & researcher
David Crosthwait:	research engineer
Maynard Marie Daly:	chemist
Annie Easley:	computer scientist

James Sylvester Gates:	theoretical physicist
Kevin Greenaugh:	nuclear engineer
Mary Jackson:	aerospace engineer
Rick Kittles:	geneticist
Samuel Kountz:	transplant surgeon
Carl Raphael Lee:	biomedical engineer
James McLurkin:	roboticist
Jerome Nriagu:	geochemist
Uzo John Uzo:	anthropologist
Hildrus Poindexter:	bacteriologist
Albert Lloyd Quarterman:	scientist
Jesse Russell:	inventor
Claude Steele:	psychologist
Henry Charles Turner:	zoologist
Dorothy Vaughan:	mathematician @ NASA
Aurthor Walker:	astronomer
Jane Wright:	cancer research
Arliner Roger Young:	zoologist

The United Negro Fund was launched in 1972, and as of 2018 has raised $2.2 billion and helped graduate more than 350,000 minority students from college.

"Stop acting white!" PLEASE!

Such an excuse for those too lazy to put the time and effort to get on the road of success and reasonable happiness.

HELEN KELLER's TEACHER ARRESTED BY CHILD SERVICES

In 1887, Anne Sullivan took the job of teaching a 7 year old girl, Helen Keller, who had been struck blind 19 months earlier in Tuscumbia Alabama. Ms. Keller was blind, deaf, unruly and spoiled. Helen's parents overindulged the child and held unbridled pity for the child.

The "The Miracle Worker," movie, about Sullivan and Keller wins an academy award in 1962.

During dinner, Helen walks around the dinner table taking food from others plates without objection, until she takes food from Ms. Sullivan's plate. Teacher Sullivan grabs Helen by the wrists and the family flies into a rage.

The family says to the new teacher, "Have you no pity on this child?"

Ms. Sullivan responds, "I'll tell you what to pity, that the sun won't rise and set for Helen all her life and you tell her every day it will. What good will your pity do Captain Keller, when you're under the strawberries?"

The mother responds, "Please!"

Teacher Sullivan responds, "I does you good! It is less trouble to feel sorry for her, than to teach her anything better."

Ms. Sullivan asks the family to leave the room where she and Helen Keller have a face off of wills in the dining room. Ms. Sullivan battles to get Helen to sit in her seat, to use a spoon, and to fold a napkin. In the process, food is thrown, spat, hair is pulled and a pitcher of water is thrown.

It shows the importance of structure, order and discipline.

Sullivan later removes Helen from the family home to a cottage where she could teach Helen without interference from Helen's parents.

If Helen Keller went to a public school in America today Ms. Sullivan would be arrested by Child Services, go to jail, and lose her teaching license for her obedience tactics to help Helen Keller become a functional human being.

If Helen Keller went to school today, she would be empowered arrest Anne Sullivan, and have the right continue living a life as a blind and deaf person in silent ignorance thanks to the "pity of Departments of Education and Child Services."

Today's laws would prevent Ms. Sullivan from instituting reasonable discipline from the start. Anne Sullivan said of Helen, "There is no point in teaching language if there is no obedience."

Just as an addict's family and friends can love that person into the grave, our educational systems has taken power away from teachers, to allow children to rule the classrooms. Teachers are no longer allowed to command obedience. When administrators take the side of the children over teachers, administration's pity for children does not help the children prepare for the hard knock world of brutal reality.

In the near future when our urban youth are not able to get into college or get a decent job due to lack of education, how does unbridled pity of administrator's help the grown children then?

As Ms. Sullivan said to the Keller family applies to Departments of Education across this country, "It (pity) does you good….it is less trouble to feel sorry, than to teach her anything better?"

FAILURE:
ACCEPTANCE & RESPONSIBILITY

Accepting failure takes strength of character, honesty and humility. It provides a building block for future achievements. When we deny culpability, we rob observes of the chance to learn from our mistakes. We condemn ourselves to a lifetime pattern of avoidance and deception. Using pathetic excuses does not allow us to mature and reach our full potential. When we do not use a personal inventory of character defects, we carry the character eroding baggage int any of our individual failures ever could.

Role of Teacher

Content provision is relevant and diverse.
Monitoring student readiness and interest
Attendance monitoring
Giving and recording assignments performance
To instill learning in their students
To inspire hope in their students
To have high expectations of their students

Role of Parents

To provide an enabling environment at home
To ensure the emotional wellbeing of their child
To ensure their child's homework is done
To provide necessary materials like notebooks, etc.
To monitor the progress of the child
To encourage their child
To have reasonable expectations of their child

Teachers and parents
have a responsibility for ensuring
that every child succeeds.

Chapter 6

Teacher Diary - Reflections

SUB TEACHER ROLL CALL
HIGH SCHOOL IN
RIDGEWOOD QUEENS

Hans	Frieda	Karl
Gertrud	Wilhelm	Hildegard
Werner	Ilse	Gunter
Ursula	Stephan	Monika
Helmut	Ute	Jurgen
Ingrid	Klaus	Erika
Wolfgang	Sabine	Heinrich
Martina	Otto	Gisela
Stephanie	Elke	Uwe
Manfred	Greta	Katrin

Crank Names #4

Al Luminum

Bill Bored

Collin Sick

Ella Mentry

Jerry Mander

Homer Sexual

Otto Matik

Penny Less

Seymour Butz

Urika Garlic

WHY DIDN'T JESUS VISIT ALLENTOWN?
Circa 1974

I am in third grade
and my Sunday School teacher
from my Hamilton Park CMA Church
in Allentown Pennsylvania
is telling
a story about Jesus.

Every week I hear about places
such as
Nazareth,
Bethlehem,
Emmaus and
Egypt.

These were all towns
surrounding Allentown.

"Ms. Van Skyke,
Why didn't Jesus visit Allentown?
It is much nicer than Bethlehem!"

I had to go college
in New York to learn
about history in my county
in Pennsylvania.

The biblical names were
mission outposts to reach
Native Americans
by the followers of Jon Hus,
or the Moravian Church
to fulfill the
Great Commission
of Jesus Christ.

Education by the Decades

1950's -Uniforms, Prayer & Longer Days:
Catholic Schools were popular. Student uniforms with slacks, button down shirts and ties. Longer days (7:30am – 4:30pm). School prayer until 1952.

1960's- Speed Reading, Segregation, Science Push:
Speed reading which was debunked in the 1970's. Brown vs. Board of Ed was made in 1954, but it was not until Green vs. Kent County in 1968 that schools were ordered to desegregate.

1970's - Cuts in Funding –Vietnam War:
School funding was cut to fund the Vietnam War, and there was fear of the U.S. falling behind in math and science. Upper classmen were going to college to get out of the Vietnam War draft.

1980's – Computers & "Latchkey Kids":
Select schools received computers and with both parents working, many kids were home alone until a parent came home from work. Schools began offering school aftercare.

1990's – SMART Boards, Chromebooks & Columbine:
The chalk board became a white board with markers, and SMART Boards where you can post lessons, show images, lessons and get access to the internet. In 1991, 19% of school had computers, by 1999, 99% had computers. The Columbine School shooting that killed 15 people, changed security measures for schools across the country.

2,000's: 9/11, No Child Left Behind, Common Core & Testing Craze:

Bush's No Child Left Behind (2002) ushered in the standardized testing, and the pressure of underperforming schools caused cheating by administrators and teachers. In 2000's, President Obama pushed for Common Core, guidelines for what students should be studying at each grade level for all subjects.

2010's: Sandy Hook, Charter Schools & Transgender Bathrooms:

3.1 million students began attending charter for profit schools supposedly based strict performance goals. With Sandy Hook, Americans were forced to accept school shootings as common. School shootings were now every 74 days versus the average of 282 days in the 1970's. Also in 2016, President Obama issued guidelines sent to all school district to ensure no students, including transgender students were discriminated against. Transgender students should use bathrooms that match their gender identity.

2020's Prediction - Computers and robots replace Administration and Teachers Get More Autonomy and More Respect as Professionals. Cell Phones become illegal in schools and students start valuing education and begin standing and bowing to the tseacher as he/she enters the classroom as students in England, India and Asia do.

Don't judge me for having goals and dreams.

STAGES OF LIFE

Who Am I? **[1-20]**   It took me to age 44 to figure out who I was….and that is okay.

Climbing the Career Ladder [21-29]   While I was never really comfortable in my own skin, climbing the career ladder in ministry, then as a Social Studies teacher, I was able to keep busy, feel good about doing, but not about being.

There are No Absolutes [30-35]   The only absolute I know of is there is a God, and I am not God.   Spending time studying religion, ethics, theology, history and psychology, I thought I had a pretty good grasp at living life.   As a evangelical, getting a divorce pretty much helped me get close to bottom.   The days of ministry are over, no church board will want a divorced leader.

Mid-Life Crisis: Entering the Cave [36-45]   Having my heart crushed by the woman of my dreams gets me into the cave. Joseph Campbell says, "The cave you fear to enter, holds your answer." Psychologist Carl Jung said, "The only way out of pain, is through the pain." Learning to face problems and pain head on is mature, and the best way to live an emotionally healthy life.

Mid-Life Resolution - The Best Years [46-50] Through the rooms, or the 12 step program, I learn to identify feelings and to sit with them instead of running and using addiction as a way to cover those feelings. I learn to become present, and my relationships with family and friends have become deeper and healthier.

Mellowing: Friends & Privacy are Important [51 on]
Who are you?
I am a son, brother, uncle, teacher, human rights activist, minister and a teacher.
That is not who you are; that is what you do. Are you a human doing or a human being?

I have learned how to be. I do not have to be a workaholic. Today I can sit at home, not do a thing, and not feel guilty about doing nothing and say, "I had a great day."

I have finally do not run from pain and feelings. I am open to learning the lessons life has been teaching me.

I am comfortable in my own skin, and I own my power today. I am not perfect, but I am excellent.

I use to hate being by myself, but today, as my own best friend, I have learned to enjoy my own company. Today I enjoy it so much, I can sometimes find myself isolating.

Balance in everything.

> I am joy.
> I am peace.
> I am a child of God.

I am.

Confession 63

<u>Jersey City Day Laborers
circa the winter of 2019</u>

Twice a month during
the work day,
I treat myself to a
$1 McDonald's coffee
and Egg McMuffin.

When Micky D's
runs the
$1 special for a
second sandwich

I buy one
and give it to
the homeless guy
on the corner or one
of the undocumented
day laborers standing
by the mall entryway.

    It is it part
    of my tithe and
        the pay off
        is the grateful
            smile on s
            human mug.

Cell Phones

The high school ladies
with purple hair were
escorted to their table
by the Diner Hostess.

The girls sad down,
looked at the menus and
then at their cell phones
before and after
placing their order with the waitress
and while they
consumed their lunch.

They looked at their cell phones
while they waited for their check
and only stopped looking at the cell phones
when they donned their jackets
and left a tip on the table.

As the Diner hipsters
exited the Diner,
one said to the other,
"Good talk!"

Zip-Zip-Zip

Attending Union Terrace Elementary
In the first half of the 1970's,
I am dancing to the song" One"
by Three Dog Night
at my 2nd grade Halloween celebration,

I could make my teacher Ms. Sotak laugh and laugh.
It felt good as a 7 year old to have some power
over an adult who graded my
math, language skills and classroom behavior
four times a year.

One day in the hallway on the way to the cafeteria,
I kept hearing this whisper of a sound
"zip, zip, zip, zip" as Ms. Sotak
escorted her 2nd grade class down to the cafeteria.
I could never figure out where the sound came from.

In 2019 as a teacher in my 19th year
as I walk down the hallway of METS Charter School
Jersey City Campus, I hear the
whisper of the "zip, zip, zip, zip."
I am brought back to the hallways of elementary school
boy days and REALIZE the whisper
is coming from between my thighs in my corduroy pants
rubbing against each other.

I will join Weight Watchers or become
the next victim of spontaneous combustion.

Rib-up, Rib-up
May 25, 2022   5:30 a.m.

I stand in the
back of my property
facing the woods
before my morning work commute,
and hear a noise.

It sounds like "rib-up"
of a frog
I have never heard before.

I stand silently
and listen waiting
for the noise.

Tens seconds later,
I
hear it.

It is the sound
from my
rumbling stomach.

Mystery solved.

The Innocents in Jail

Research
Shows
4%
of the
incarcerated
are
innocent.

That
comes
to 90,000
wrongly
imprisoned
Americans.
The
Shawshank
Redemption
Movie
is
the
scariest
horror
movie
to
me.

PUBLIC SCHOOL PRAYER DISSONANCE 2018

Mr. Geist, I think our country, school and education system would be better if we could have prayer in school. Ever since the Atheists took prayer to the Supreme Court to have it removed, our country is going to school to hell in a hand basket.

Okay Jimmy Baker Junior, even though in Engel vs. Vitale (6-25-62), the Supreme Court ruled having prayer in school was a violation of the 1st Amendment because it is considered "establishment of religion." Okay Jimmy Baker Junior, for you, I will open our class today in prayer.

Everyone quiet down, close your eyes - or not…here we go – 5-4-3-2-1……

Dear Buddha, please help us to be in Zen state of mind today…..

NO, NO, NO!!! Not to Buddha Mr. G!
Sorry. Okay, here we go again…

Dear Allah, please help us to follow the five pillars to the best of….

NO, NO, NO!!! Are you crazy? That is the religion of the enemy terrorist fundamentalists!
Sorry - this is not easy. Close your eyes everyone.

Dear 10,000 Gods of Hinduism….
NO, NO, NO!!! There is only one God Mister!
Sorry. This is not easy this school prayer stuff. Give me another chance.

Dear God of Atheism, please help us to not keep the faith…

NO, NO, NO!!! Atheists do not believe in God - this prayer is not logically possible. How do you pray to something you don't believe in?
Good point Jimmy Baker Junior. All right, all right. I got it this time.

"Dear Satan, may all teachers parish on their annual plane ride to the teacher convention on the West Coast. Amen."

SILENCE.

Class? Billy? Oh I see, not having to go to school is more important than having school prayer. I DON'T LIKE THAT PRAYER. Let me try another one.

Dear God, or Higher Power of our choosing, whether it is a traditional God, or the group conscience, or the banana for lunch on my desk, please help us to….

NO, NO, NO!!! What is this Higher Power crap? May I say the prayer Mr. Geist?

Go ahead Jimmy.

Dear God of our Lord Jesus Christ, not the white one with blue eyes, or the black Malcolm X Muhammad Ali looking Jesus, but a Middle Eastern Looking one....

THE CLASS CHIMES IN - NO, NO, NO JIMMY BAKER JUNIOR. We live in a pluralistic society and you cannot just call out one God, for we all have different beliefs which helps make our heterogeneous society great.

"Class, see why we do not have prayer in school. Just know this, as long as schools have testing in school, there will always be school prayer. Carry on."

School Prayer Led By A Student
Billy Bob McSillyBilly

Dear God,

Please make the week go quickly to get us to the weekend.

Please give illness to Ms. McGillacutty, I did not study for my algebra exam today.

Please may we not have liver today for lunch.

Please let may the cafeteria serve us tater tots every day until the end of the year.

Please let it snow tomorrow, I don't want to work on my social studies paper tonight.

Please have Sally, the annoying girl with freckles, stop crushing on me.

Please have Bonnie, the head cheer leader crush on me.

Please help me get on the baseball team this Spring.

OH…and please God bless our country, and our Philadelphia Eagles, Phillies, Flyers and 76ers.

Amen.

CIVIC CLASS and SUFFRAGE

When our country started,
not every white man could vote.
Only white men
who owned property could.

In my civic classes,
we talk about how the South
disenfranchised people of color
from voting by using
the Grandfather clause,
poll taxes, and
reading tests.

Every year when I ask for a show
of hands how many students
support the suffrage of woman,
the students get a "whhaaatttt"
look in their eyes.

The students confuse
the word suffering
with suffrage.
Of course, suffrage is
the right to vote,
not the right to
physically abuse women

I think today, voters should have
to pass "the suffrage word test"
before being able to vote.
      # Me Too.

NYC COUNCILMAN MIGUEL MARTINEZ
Circa 2007

Teaching a Government Class in Washington Heights, I invited their Councilman to come and speak with the students about Civics. Councilman Miguel Martinez never responded to the e-mail or phone calls. He and his cherry pie smile did show up at our graduation to give a speech.

As he exits, I stick out my hand and when he shakes it, I do not let go.

Hello Councilman. My name is Mr. Geist.

"Oh, you are the Social Studies teacher from the High School of Health Careers and Sciences. I am sorry I never got back to you."

Mr. Councilman, let me be clear. If you do not come and visit the children of your constituents next year, I will make sure you are not allowed to speak at the next graduation.

"Mr. Geist. Please give me a call, and I will come to speak to your class next school year."

The following year, I call, and e-mail and get no response from NYC Councilman Miguel Martinez.

This is called a "teachable moment," and I explain to the class how the Councilman lied to us and is ignoring us.

I write his office number on the black board and say, "Class, if you want the Councilman to visit us, keep calling this phone number until his office gets back to me."

His office gets back to me and says, "Mr. Geist, can you please tell your class to stop calling our office. We will come to the class next week."

Our class comes up questions for the Councilman, and suggestions on how to improve the neighborhood. The visit is a success, and Miguel is impressed with the conversation with the kids.

In 2009 Councilman Martinez is arrested and convicted of embezzling $106,000 from a community fund and sent to prison for 5 years.

The Councilman should have been nice to us. He would have received more Christmas cards at Cell Block D, Cell #324.

LOOKING FOR SOMETHING
2008

As I teach and
walk around the class,
things disappear off my desk,
usually pens and pencils,
my book or sometimes
the class notes.

In my head,
I know where
I placed something,
but when I go to retrieve
the needed item
it is gone and
it makes me feel
`nutty`.

An astute student in my
Global History class named
Abel sits in front of me and
says, "Are you looking for
something Mr. Geist?"

I say, "Why yes Abel, I am."

He responds,
"Are you looking for your
dignity?" as he holds my
blue pen I am looking for.

Dear Senator Booker,   August 25, 2016

I was a pastor in NYC for 5 years, grew up in a UAW & 1199 union home, and was a UFT member for 13 years and worked two years in Newark.

Thank-you for your work on prison reform in our country and I hope you work on making medical marijuana legal and recreational to cut down on the prison population and as a way to raise tax money.

CHARTER SCHOOLS:
In the Atlantic Magazine, it is reported you said as Newark Mayor, you wanted to make Newark the charter capital of the world.

I worked at **Newark Leadership Academy** on 301 West Kinney St., and THERE WAS NO DISCIPLINE CONSEQUENCES. Students knew they would get a meeting with a counselor, with no real consequences. I ended up getting assaulted there. The motto of Principal and A.P. was, "Don't call us unless there is a knife, gun or blood on the floor."

The following year I worked at **Merit Prep Charter** across from the City Hall at 909 Broadway. The deans were excellent, but like the other school, the students have more power than the teachers. Every student has a lap top, and many were playing video games and listening to music during most of my class. I held the kids accountable to do their work, so they just sent messages to the Principal they did not like me as a teacher. My contract was not renewed.

At my end of the year review my teaching coach said, "Mr. Geist, you are a professional, you know your content, and you implemented my suggestions." The Principal said, "Yeaaaaaa, but the kids did not like you. We have to let you go."

My experience with charters is they are not better than the NYC public schools I worked for, and in fact, they were experiments in keeping kids busy while using grade rubrics that are a joke. At Merit Prep, a 75 was an A, and anything above a 35 was passing. This is helping prepare kids for college?

CHARTERS ARE ABOUT UNION BUSTING:
I read a study in 2001 that said only 23% of charters do better than public schools. Other studies show the best schools in the country have teacher unions.

Is your position on charters still the same?

Sincerely,
Jim Geist
Hewitt NJ

Note: I never received a response from Senator Booker's office. **Merit Charter School was closed in June of 2017 by the N.J. State.**

EVENING SCHOOL SCAM
(1999)

I teach Night School at Park West High in NYC
for five semesters or two and a half years.
The extra 3,000 clams a semester helps pay the
mortgage payments.

I taught one summer school class,
HOT, no air conditioning,
crowded and difficult to teach with
the large noisy six foot metal fan running.
The fan was almost as big as
a propeller on a Florida swamp boat.

On my first night of teaching 50 kids
show up and 20 are standing in the class.
I tell the students they must write a 20 page
paper for the Economics class to pass.
The next class two days later, 30 show up.

I overhear a group of students
during day school say,
"It does not matter if you fail a class,
Just make it up in summer or evening school."
I realize that night school and evening school
contribute to students not taking day school
seriously.

In 2016, I work at a school in Newark.
a counselor named Maria walks up to me
and says, "Did you teach night school at Park West?"
I say yes. It is seventeen years later and
I am working with a former student of mine.

Am I "officially" old now?

ELKS LODGE BEAUTY CONTEST
(circa 2015)

The pork chops, sour kraut and

mashed potato dinner is filling.

The rock band is fairly good.

The square bar is full of round people

as I sit at a small high table

against the back wall with Tiffany.

She is a blond with blue eyes and shapely.

A drunk woman passes us

on the way to the bathroom,

she points at Tiffany and says,

"You are beautiful."

The drunk points at me,

Loses her smile and says,

"You are okay looking."

The drunk says what

the sober person thinks.

SOLUTION TO AMERICAN EDUCATION

Education, education, education…we are falling behind the rest of the world! Teachers and teacher unions are the problem. The children – who will speak up for the children?!?!?! I know the solution, but apparently it is something our Supreme Court has frowned upon.

How lucky for the justices to sit in their quiet chambers reading recommendations from their clerks regarding cases, being alone with their thoughts, papers and classical music and sipping their coffees or herbal tea that may or may not have a hit of whiskey in it, attending their weekly Thursday Night first amendment pornography viewing evenings hosted by Justice Clarence Thomas.

School was different when Justice Oldie Fogies went to school, but they have not been in a classroom in the South Bronx, Newark, or any urban place or suburban school– in the last four decades. Teachers used to be captains of the classrooms.

GEIST v. NEWARK SCHOOL DISTRICT (2014)

While Mr. Geist, a former pastor and Teacher of the Year may be correct that being able to use a Taser gun or cattle prod on one incorrigible student per semester would bring considerable positive behavioral change in the young people who may have not received proper home training for various reasons, backed by the science of the impact of poverty and P.T.S.D. we the Court of the United States of America, the interpreters of what is deemed constitutional or not, have decided by a 6-2 decision, that such class room management control being truly effective for the sake of the majority children, must suffer at the hands of the 3-4 knuckleheads in class that have no respect for their teachers giving them tools to live a life of reasonable happiness, and the opportunity to climb the ladder of success in life by building reading, writing, and reasoning skills.

Might does not make right for citizens, but especially teachers who are some of the last to still have union representation. Might for right is only for corporations, the military and the Congress, Senate and President.

Unfortunately, the majority must suffer, despite the fact that any juvenile delinquents would think twice before acting knowing they could end up on the floor with their tongues hanging out until they re-gain their senses with students standing around them laughing and pointing at the incapacitated trouble maker.

How much better would it be in the classrooms if teachers could teach, and decent students would be able to learn without constant talking, disrespectful behavior and frequent interruptions during class instruction.

Talking back to the teacher, using the "n" word, playing videos and music on cell phones and the right to interrupt class is an American right. No wonder foreign exchange students jaws are on the ground in every class they attend. I guess the military basic training could be next – yelling at a student is now considered corporal punishment.

Taser guns are "cruel and unusual punishment in the classroom," and class bullying is a protected right.

*The information conveyed in this piece
may or may not be totally true.*

Good Master

In 2002 I dated a
Chinese woman named Huan.
It was pronounced Juan,
but I called her
Huuuuuu-aaaaaaaan.
She did not seem to mind.

Huan was tall,
liked badminton and
ball room dancing.
From her I learned
how to say "thank-you"
in Chinese - "Shea-shea"

I once had guests over
to my Queens apartment
and Huan said,
"Jim is a good master."
It felt weird because slavery
had been illegal for over 130 years,
moreover,
I had been the NYC director of the
American Anti-Slavery Group
from 1996-2002.

By "master,"
Huan really meant
teacher.

BLAME THE TEACHER

Blaming a teacher for the behavior of a disrespectful students in class IS AS LUDICROUS AS...

Blaming a doctor for illness or

Blaming the fireman for the raging fire or

Blaming the police for bank robbers or

Blaming the dentist for your tooth ache or

Blaming the psychologist for your mental illness or

Blaming the preacher for your sin or

Blaming the painter for a home not painted for 20 years or

Blaming the plumber for your sink getting clogged up or

Blaming the mechanic for your blown engine or

Blaming the scientist for natural disasters or

Blaming the garbageman for your messy house.

If children do not come from stable homes or from families that value education, it is almost impossible for a teacher to motivate them to do classwork and homework in the pursuit of building reading, writing and critical thinking skills.

Teaching is like trying to capture the attention of a class full of squirrels. It is easier rounding up 100 cats.

I HAVE BEEN TO ALLENTOWN TOO
(circa 1992 – Rockland County NY)

I am sitting on a 5 gallon plastic
paint bucket during lunch break
with the crew from
Rockland Painting.

Chris says, "Jim,
I hear you are from
Allentown Pennsylvania.
I have been to
Allentown as well!

I was hanging out
with my drinking buddies
and got so drunk
I jumped 200 feet into
a quarry lake and
broke my back on impact.

A Medivac Helicopter flew
me to the Lehigh Valley
Hospital in Allentown."

My mouth is agape.

Chris goes on,
"I have been to Allentown –
Don't remember the jump,
breaking my back,
or the helicopter ride."

Most visitors coming
to Allentown is
for Dorney Park.

I am quite sure…

attending the
Amusement Park
in a sober state
of mind is more
fun than being in
a body cast for
six months.

TEACHER OBITUARY
(circa 2005)

I was visiting my folks
in Pennsylvania in
August of 2005.

In the early morning
as I sat on the back porch
drinking my coffee,
I felt the urge,
a burning desire to
peruse the obituary
section of the Morning Call
this particular Saturday.

I turn to the obit page
And there is a picture
Of Ms. McGuirren and
Mr. Kotran,
math teachers at
Raub Junior High School
From 1978-1980.

They both died young,
not even reaching age
to collect any of the
Social Security they paid
into their whole careers.

I tell the story to
my students and tell them

I felt some guilt
because I had misbehaved
in their classes at times.

I tell my students,
"I don't want any of you
to feel bad the morning
you are drinking your coffee
and looking over the
obituary when you see
my handsome mug in it.
I don't want you feeling
guilty about misbehaving
in my class.

DO THE RIGHT THING,
BEHAVE,
BE RESPECTFUL,
do your work
and on my passing,
you will feel no guilt."

The behavior
motivation
works for less
than 10 minutes.

The Patience Wore Thin

I started working for the Jersey City Board of Education in September of 2021. The commute is 90 minutes. It takes 30 minutes to get from Hewitt to Oakland on Route 287, then it take ½ hour from Oakland NJ to drive into Jersey City en Route

At the hour mark of my work pilgrimage, I stop by McDonald's to purchase my coffee regular (2 cream & 2 sugars for the non-NYC metropolitan folk), for $1.07. After getting my coffee, I have another ½ hour drive through Jersey City until I pull up to Innovation High School.

Donuts to dollars, a McDonald's cup of coffee is a better cup of coffee compared to the Dunkin Donuts swill. Picking up a cup of coffee gives me a chance to stretch my legs, and to meet some of the locals and to get a smile and a "have a nice day!"

Daily, a man drives his wife to McDonald's where she picks up her breakfast. I am no expert on mental health. She is an older lady, whose hair is usually disheveled, has a gimp walk that goes with it.

She looked like a crazy-cat lady, but I have no

idea if she owns cats. While Steve Martin was the "wild and crazy guy," she was might have been crazy, but there was no sign of sense of humor.

Should I say she was "touched?" Is it better to say "a person with a mental illness?"

On this day, she is ahead of me. I have placed my order after her, I am waiting 5 minutes for my coffee. I usually get my coffee within two minutes. The woman, who ordered ahead of me, has ordered her Egg McMuffin, hash brown and coffee is pacing back and forth. She walks up to the counter is looking especially irritated, and THEN, IT HAPPENS....

"WHERE IS MY BREAKFAST?!?! I WANT MY BREAKFAST!"

I mean she really screamed. She was hungry, dammit! She was assertive.

The seagulls hanging out on the parking lot lamp tops flew into the next county in a fit of fear.

The lady with the messy hair and smeared lip stick gets her breakfast.

I get my coffee -
        and a short story.

YELLING MATCH WITH GOD
(like Jonah)   10/4/21

I was unemployed for 14 months. Merit Prep Charter School was closed by the state of New Jersey June 30th of 2020. Students were sad; they really loved this school. Even some teachers cried. Not me – been through this and rolled up my shirt sleeves for the new job hunt.

In March of 2020, due to Covid, we switched over to Zoom Teaching. It was a strange time for the teachers. I taught at three charter schools, and Merit Prep was the best of the charter schools I worked at. Many teachers were sad, a young pretty blond told me, "I don't care if they close it down, I will just find another job."

If you are young, or if you are young and pretty, then you will get hired quickly. I was aged 53. I will never forget when a retired teacher, who was working as a substitute teacher said to me, "If you are over 50, you will never get hired as a teacher in a new school district."

For fourteen months, I sent out hundreds of resumes, and was invited to a dozen interviews. Most of the times I was told, "You were our second choice. If things don't work out, we will get back to you."

Biden was sworn in as President January of 2021. Unemployment is usually collected for 6 months. With the Covid Pandemic, it was extended twice. The America Cares Act was passed, which meant if you lost your job in the time of Covid, the foreclosure of your home could not be initiated for 18 months after missing your first mortgage payment.

Long story short, I started working in the Jersey City School District in September of 2021. I was hired at a middle school in the Greenville section of the city. I will not mention the name of the school, but will say, there were no consequences for poor behavior. If there is no detention, where is the incentive to listen to your teacher? When students care less about grades, you are screwed.

I taught 6th grade. My classroom had no smart board. I could not project my lessons, videos, or images. The students refused to follow the seating chart, which made it difficult to learn student names. Students did not do their work, students walked around the class, and talked with each other and would act as if I was invisible.

Students would eat chips, drink soda, take the bottles of hand sanitizer and spray them desks or on the classroom walls.

Students would walk in or out of class when they wanted. They would not honor the bathroom pass, they just got up and went when they wanted, and I had a group of 5-6 girls who would run out and go to the bathroom at the same time AND THERE WAS NO DETENTION GIVEN IN THE SCHOOL.

It was frustrating, demeaning, and was giving me gray hair and the shakes. At dinner, my hands were visibly shaking. In all my years of teaching, rarely did I ever get a headache. This place gave me migraines!

I don't fully blame the kids, I blame the adults in charge of the school. I blame the C.I.T., or Crisis Intervention Teacher, who I was told, always responded to inappropriate behavior of students with "THAT does not fit the definition of crisis."

Every day I prayed the Serenity Prayer. "God, grant me the serenity to accept the things I cannot change, the courage to change the things I can; and the wisdom to know the difference."

On October 4th, of 2021, on my 1.5 hour commute to work, on the Route 78 Bridge over the Newark Bay, I began screaming, as the famous argument Jonah had with God.

"God, why do I always end up working in difficult schools!?! I have always given my best to the students. When will I be able to get into a decent school? When will I get motivated students who want an education and have an adequate amount of respect for teachers! I am sad! I am frustrated! I am angry! Are you listening? Do you care?"

Tuesday October 5th, 2021: I get an e-mail from the Principal. He says, "Mr. Geist, as of Friday, you will no longer be with us."

WHAT? Am I getting fired?

"No Mr. Geist – you will be moving to a high school. You will be moving to one of Jersey City's best high schools."

Can you tell me why?

"Mr. Geist - just look at this as a promotion. Congratulations! I wish you the best! Don't mess up. This is your chance to shine."

On my way home, as I cross over the Newark Bay Bridge, I say to God, "You listened. Thank you!"

I am grateful for Innovation High School and the opportunity to teach there. As a lottery school, for every three students who apply, one will be accepted – and this makes all the difference.

FLAT TIRE

I have a B.J.'s membership; I buy my tires here. In the fall, I have my winter tires mounted on my vehicles. In the Spring, I switch back to the all season tires. Every other gas fill-up, I put air in my tires. I cannot believe how much of my life is dedicated to auto tires.

I can still hear my 9th grade chemistry teacher, Mr. Lochner say, "What does a car ride on?" Students give answer such as axels, tires or rubber, and Mr. Lochner in a smart aleck voice says, "NO - air!"

On my commute to Jersey City, I feel my front tire is not riding correctly. I am on Route 3 on the way towards NYC on a 3 lane highway of autos driving likes hounds on their way to hell. The Manhattan skylight in the sunrise looks as the backdrop of Oz in the 1978 movie, "Wizard of Oz."

I get from the left lane to the right lane and pull into the first gas station I can find, that happens to be a Gulf Station. It is frigid November day, and I take off the flat tire, now ruined, and put on a donut tire on the 2016 black Ford C-Max hybrid.

I drive to school with my mitts covered in grime and tire and tire rub marks, scuffs and that tire smell.

After school, I stop by the closest tire/auto store, that is on a busy corners, and is full of vehicles. There is one spot to park in, and I back the car in so I can make a quick and safe exit.

As I put the gear into park, a Ford Bronco beeps loud and long to let me know of his displeasure. It is a large man, and he is black and angry. He is Wesley Snipes -Barry White black.

I say, "Calm down buddy. We all need to get our autos serviced - and I will be out of here in one minute."

"I need to get out of the lot!"
"So do I, in one minute. I appreciate your patience."

I give my flattened tire to the mechanic, and tell him I will pick up the fixed tire the next day (which I do for $80).

I get in the C-Max with my donut tire affixed, and wave to the angry Barry White character as I pull out towards Route 78 West back to West Milford New Jersey.

I could see in my rear mirror Barry yelling something.

I think the man in the Bronco was saying,

"We got it together didn't we? Isn't it nice, my kind of wonderful. The first, my last, my everything."

Not.

UNION TOBACCO

Nana Geist smoked cigarettes. Every once in a while, I smell the cigarette smoke and ask, "Is that you Nana? I love you and miss you."

Grandpa Short smoked Union Tobacco in his pipe. Any family dinner, he would go to the back porch, take his tobacco pipe bag, and smoke his Union Tobacco. Every once in a while, I smell the tobacco smell, and I ask, "Is that you Grandpa? I love you and miss you."

When Grandpa Short passed, one of the things I took was a small metal container of Archer's Lin Seed Oil. Grandpa told me, every Spring, I take a rag with Lin Seed Oil, and rub it over the tools in the garage and gardening tools. I LOVE THE SMELL OF LIN SEED OIL!

One of my Spring rituals is to clean my tools and gardening tools with the Lin Seed Oil. I always feels Grandpa's presence when I do this.

I sometimes tear up, but I laugh more often at the memories of loved ones as time wears on. People come into your life for a day, a season, or a lifetime I have heard.

In approximately 2008, my parents let me borrow their dog, Chesca, half black lab and half border collie. She was smart, and obedient, and always stayed 15 feet of her owners when going on a walk with no leash.

She shadowed me as I did my yard work, painting and invited friends over for a summer party. As I gathered fire wood for the camp fire, she followed me back and forth, back and forth, with her tongue out, and her tail wagging, so happy to be a dog on a perfect blue skied day.

Chesca passed in approximately 2010. My parents will never get another dog, because it was so painful to lose what felt to be a family member. Grandpa Short use to say, "Chesca is more human, than many humans."

In the Spring of 2020, as I am blasting music from the radio, and gathering wood behind my home for the campfire, I notice a monarch butterfly shadowing me.

This butterfly, is following me from the woods, to the campfire area, back to the woods and back to the campfire area. I have a butterfly following me, just as Chesca did back in 2008. I am filled with gratefulness for having such a wonderful dog the families life, introduced by my sister Jody.

I stop, and the butterfly lands on a flower next to me.

I say, "Chesca, Is that you? I love you and miss you."

5th Grade Trip to Philadelphia
1976

It is a Union Terrace Elementary trip to visit Constitution Hall and the Liberty Bell. Students meet at the school, load on the bus to visit the City of Brotherly Love in the year of our Bicentennial.

I have never been, so I look forward to being in the city of our beloved Eagles, Phillies, 76ers, Flyers and Rocky Balboa. On the trip down, students are talking about 5th grade stuff, and what they are going to eat for lunch. I have my ham and cheese sandwich and carrot sticks; I am jealous of those who brought hoagies or pizza with them.

We tour Constitution Hall. I find it boring. It We see the Liberty Bell with its crack, and then go to the park to eat our lunches on this sunny day sitting on green wooden benches and concrete walls of the water fountain that day before heading back to Allentown.

The pigeons, sparrows and squirrels beg and bother us using telepathic communication to get us to throw them crumbs. As we are leaving, I see several older men with beards, going through the garbage cans, and eating what leftovers we have left behind. Ewe! Revolting! I am horrified. WE HAVE HOMELESS IN AMERICA?

What I remember most about the trip, is homeless and hungry people. The trip is a reality enema. How does this happen in the land of the brave, free and bountiful? This will be the first of many more disappointments this young man will learn about the reality of the "greatest country on earth."

KILLERS – CLASS OF 1984

I attend an alum's restaurant
in Allentown with
three fellow graduates.
It has been over 30 years
since we graduated.

I think back to the graduation
convocation in 1984, the themes
of speeches given by students,
teachers, administrators and some
windbag politicians.

It is tough to stay focused in a
gymnasium oven full of June
summer temperature with a mixture
of humidity and body heat.

> Life is a journey…
> Never give up…
> Never forget where you came from…
> Change the world…
> Follow your dreams…

I have not lived in the
Lehigh Valley for 25 years -
I am out of the gossip loop.

I bring my Comus Yearbook and
my two friends begin paging
through the senior pictures
of the 700 fellow Canaries

I graduated with.

Lanie and Bill begin pointing at different pictures of senior with their 80's culture of mullets, punk cuts, big hair and perms as they begin the commentary.

> Owns business xyz,
> drunk,
> famous clothing designer,
> hooker,
> actor,
> in jail,
> writer,
> suicide,
> gay,
> NFL player,
> dead,
> pilot,
> pedophile,
> rapist,
> murderer.

Imagine that, of the 700 graduates, two males killed girlfriends and one killed is wife. One even used an ax to cut up the girlfriend to try to make it easier to get her into garbage bags.

If you graduated in my class
As a male, there was
a 1/120th chance you
could end up being a murderer.

These were not things I would
have equated with school spirit
or with setting life goals.

If I ever get invited to give
a commencement speech,
it will be memorable, truthful,
and probably the last one
I am ever invited to give.

*Can you image where you will
be 30 years from now?*

*Here are
a few possibilities
besides the stories
of the
shiny
successful
graduate
stories.*

VARSITY PRINTING TEAM
Circa 1981

In 1981 at William Allen High School in the printing department, a student makes a money tree for an Uncle, and uscs printing shop machines to created $5 dollar bills for the money tree.

In February of 1981, the Secret Service show up to investigate who was creating fuzzy $1 and $5 bills that were turning up at the local arcade, pizza shops and downtown 6th Street hooker circuit. It turns out a 17 year old had printed approximately $11,000 of counterfeit money. Why work for your money when you can let your counterfeited money work for you?

The news makes the Allentown Morning Call, and went national in Time Magazine and even lands as a joke on the Johnny Carson Show.

Labor is the amount of time spent making money that represents the value of goods and services. Counterfeiting is theft and undercuts the value of money. You are receiving goods and services, without having put in your time in labor for the value of the goods and services. There is a reason work is called work – it takes energy to make a living.

The following year, t-shirts are printed up at the William Allen High School saying "Varsity Printing Team," and on the backs have the image of a $5 bill. That is funny.

WASHING MY SHOES
Spring of 1973

I am aged 8 in third grade with Ms. Ott. She has blond hair and eye glasses, and sometimes is very moody. On this Spring day at the 3pm release time, I begin my 3 mile walk home in my dress shoes.

Next to Union Terrace Elementary is the Union Terrace Pond. I walk along the pond with my hard plastic bottomed dress shoes, and slip on the mud and take end up in the pond. I land on my feet, and I am in one foot of water. It is as if the pond contains a large magnet in the lake, and my shoes were made out of nickel, iron and cobolt and pulled me right in.

As I am walking along the edge of the pond, a yellow pick-up truck with the Allentown Pennsylvania insignia pulls along the sidewalk, and I look to see it is my Uncle Fritz who is driving it. Uncle Fritz is a city worker and the family clown, and for sure, this story is going to be shared with my eight pairs of Aunts and Uncles and dozens of cousins at Nana Geist's house this coming Sunday.

"Jimmy, what are you doing? Why are you in the Union Terrace Pond in your dress clothes?"
I answer, *"What do you think? I am washing my be-damn shoes!"*

THIS story I must endure for the rest of my life at every Geist Christmas Family Party and Uncle Fritz laughs and wheezes every time. When I think back, such a witty and snarky answer for an eight year old to give his smart aleck Uncle.

MOCKED

Teaching 6th graders history in Newark circa 2016, a young lady walks up to my teacher desk and says in a mocking voice, "Mr. Geist, I bet you did not know Christians are suffering persecution in many countries throughout the world – ***did you***?"

Little did she know from 1997 through 2,000, most of my free time was dedicated to educating people about the persecution of Christians in Islamic and Communist countries. I had organized a coalition advocacy group in NYC called the Interfaith Alliance for Christian Human Rights made up of 50 organizations.

In 1998 and 1999, I was the NYC director of the International Day of Prayer held on the second Sunday every November. It was a way of educating American Christians about what their brothers and sisters were suffering for the sole act of believing in Jesus Christ as their Savior.

I organized demonstrations in front of the Egyptian Consulate and Sudanese Consulates in NYC. I had been interviewed in eight radio interviews, spoke two television cable shows and had meetings with

NYC Council Speaker Peter Vallone and many calls and letters to the local Congress people. I spoke at forums at colleges, high schools and churches in New York, New Jersey and Pennsylvania. I had also helped spark newspaper articles, radio and news television news pieces.

Our group lobbied for the International Religious Freedom Act which passed in 1998 in the Congress which:

1) Created an Ambassador-at-Large for International Religious Freedom in the Department of State

2) A bi-partisan U.S. Commission on International Religious Freedom

3) A Special Adviser on International Religious Freedom within the National Security Council.

I often spoke of the genocide and modern day slavery happening in Sudan. Over a million Sudanese had been killed, but most Americans did not care because they were black Africans.
In the Bosnian genocide, as the Muslims were being killed, President Clinton and N.A.T.O

became involved in an aerial bombing campaign to the genocide of the Muslim population, which was white.

I organized a rally on behalf of Sudanese in front of the United Nations for Saturday September 15th in 2001, but was called by the NYC police on September 12th informing our permit for the rally had been declined in light of the 9/11 attack.

I was as a minister at New Life Fellowship in Elmhurst Queens, and my wife informed me she wanted a divorce. She said "YOU love slaves and persecuted Christians more than me!" What I learned from many involved in human rights advocacy was their relationships often suffered separations, break-ups and divorce. My divorce became final two weeks after the 9/11/01 terrorist attack in NYC and Washington D.C.

When Letisha the sixth grader asked me in a mocking way if I knew that Christians were being persecuted in many parts of the world, I held my tongue, and took time to stop and breathe. I answered Letisha, "I am aware of the persecution and I want to thank you for asking me if I was aware of it. Thanks for sharing, and keep sharing the what you know with others."

JOBS OVER MY LIFETIME

Dishes/Trash	House Painting
Paper Boy	Driver to Airport
Lemonade Stand	Mover (1 day)
Yard Sales	**Deck Staining**
Snow Shoveling	Power Washer
Raking Leaves	United Parcels Service Loader
Graveyard Security	Selling Frozen Shrimp (1 day)
Sealing Driveways	**Youth Pastor**
Junk Removal	*Collecting Unemployment*
House Sitting	Roofer (1 day)
Dog Walking	Pastor in NYC
Baby Sitting	Substitute Teacher
Carpenter Assistant	**Landlord**
College Kitchen Janitor	**History Teacher**
Sunday School Teacher	Detention Room Monitor
House Cleaning	E-Bay Seller
Conference Speaker	**Author**

bold = jobs enjoyed

IS GEEST HERE?

The first day of school from elementary through secondary school, including every semester of college and graduate school, when taking attendance the teacher or professor would often say,

"Is James here? James GEEST?

"No, my last name is pronounced Geist,
with the long I (eye)
as in Poltergeist"

In my German class in 8th grade
Frau Sandt taught us:

"ei" sounds like "i" and
"ie" sounds like "e."

I am half German,
and received a D in
German class.

Frau Sandt may have given me
a "D" in middle school,
but she knew how to
pronounce my
last name.

DISCOVERY IS MORALLY NEUTRAL

The <u>Anarchist Handbook</u> has been found in the hands of alienated young people who have launched attacks on classmates and teachers. . .the continued publication of the Cookbook serves no purpose but other than a commercial one for the publisher. It should quickly and quietly go out of print.

-author ***William Powell***

To atone for this accomplishment [of the creation of dynamite used bombs in warfare] and to relieve his conscience, ***Alfred Nobel*** instituted an award for the promotion of peace.

-Albert Einstein

Robert Oppenheimer who helped in the creation of the Atomic Bomb told President Truman, "Mr. President, I feel I have blood on my hands." Truman said, "The blood is on my hands, let me worry about it."

Mikhail Kalashnikov, developer of the AK-47 automatic assault rifle found it painful when his weapon was used in criminal activities. "The spiritual pain is unbearable - how can it be that I...a Christian and Russian Orthodox believer is to blame for people's deaths?"

Progress.

THE PRICE OF TRUTH TELLING

The Old Testament Prophets

Jesus

John Brown

President Abraham Lincoln

Pontiac

The Molly Maguires

Governor Huey Long

Gandhi

Malcolm X

John F. Kennedy

Martin Luther King

Bobby Kennedy

Harvey Milk

Karen Silkwood

Bishop Oscar Romero

Those who challenge the power structures
often expire early.

MEMORIAL SERVICE: JAMES C. GEIST
future date to be determined by God

Greeting and Opening Prayer

First Reading: 2nd Corinthians 4:13 – 5:1
Second Reading: Revelation 21: 1-7

Reading of **Obituary**
Hymn: How Great Thou Art (verses 1,2 &4)

Prayer of St. Francis (Channel of Peace)
Eulogy (two friends)

Song: Where Does the Time Go? (Judy Collins)
    -power point images of Jim's life

Third Reading: John 14:1-7
Post-Mortem **Letter from Jim to Family and Friends**

Fourth Reading: 2 Timothy 4:6-8
Apostle's Prayer:

Song: We'll Meet Again
    (sing until the end of the second refrain of)
    We'll meet again, Don't know where, don't know when,
    But I know, we'll meet again some sunny day.

<u>**RECEPTION FOLLOWING IN CHURCH BASEMENT**</u>
Jim's ashes to be spread:
1) by Hamilton Park Basketball Court,
2) Woods in front of the Tall Pines Camp,
3) from the top of his last High School at 3pm - so students become one with their teacher

Chapter 7

Bosses

SUB TEACHER ROLL CALL
HEBREW SCHOOL

Tova	Zamora	Ona
Meir	Levi	Issac
Chaya	Penina	Rivka
Noah	Gabriel	Joseph
Esther	Norah	Shana
Daniel	Elijah	Avi
Hila	Israela	Hannah
Gil	Israel	Joshua
Keren	Golda	Naomi
Ezra	Daniel	Gideon
Michaela	Breindal	Dynah
Asher	Elias	Hershel

Prank Names #5

Ann Jyna

Bud Wiser

Dinah Mite

Eric Tyle

Ginger Vitis

Hy Gene

Ray Ling

Pete Zaria

Sue E. Side

Val Crow

ELEMENTARY SCHOOL PORN
1971

The Supreme Court does not give a
specific definition for pornography – you
know what pornography is when you see it.

In the Library as I peruse Sports Illustrated,
and some National Geographic Magazines,
there is an article with pictures about a group
of people recently discovered called the Tasaday
in the Philippines, who have never met modern
people. They are called Stone Age People.
In the pics, the woman are not wearing tops.

I cannot stop staring at the breasts of the
Tasaday women. My second grade
teacher sneaks up to my table and says,
"I knew it, put that down."

My excitement turns to shame.

How can something "bad"
for viewing enjoyment be
allowed in the elementary
school library?

As Jimmy Kimmel and Adam
Carola of The Man Show
(1999-2004) answer:
"Why do men love boobs?"
is the same as asking
"Why do men breathe?"

BULLY BOSS
2003-2006

I received tenure as a NYC teacher in 2003. It was the year my Assistant Principal retired, and the new A.P., Mr. Jose Cruz took over.

A.P. Cruz was Dominican, and wore a hearing aid. He had a tough time hearing, and it was tough to communicate clearly at times.

He had a shaved head and reminded me of the actor Geoffrey Holder, the actor who use to be in the 7- Up commercials. He would say, "7-Up, the Un-cola! And then he gave a Ahhhhhh-ah-ahhhh" laugh at the end of the 1970's commercial.

Some of the teachers in the Park West High School Social Studies Department thought he was harmless or friendly. My instinct told me otherwise.

In 2005, I bought a boat to use for fishing on Upper Greenwood Lake in West Milford, and I christened the boat the name "McCruz-in," for my boss.

A.P. Cruz left Park West High to become an A.P. at Murray Bertraum High School and in the Fall of 2010 he became Principal of Technology Magnet High School in Cambria Heights. The Daily News ran an article "New Bully Principal in Queens," and it was about Principal Jose Cruz.

As of 2013, the school was under investigation by the Department of Education for extremely lenient grading of the Regents exams jumping from 54% passing to 88% passing in 2011.

He made life tough for many teachers and was nicknamed "Principal Napoleon" by the staff.

I knew that back in 2003.

SOCIAL PYRAMIDS

Japanese Feudalism
Emperor
Shogun
Daimyo
Samurai
Peasants

European Feudalism
King
Nobles
Knights
Merchants-Farmers
Peasants

Spanish Encomienda System
Peninsulares
Creoles
Mestizos/Mulattoes
Slaves – African/Natives

American Education
Superintendents
Principals – A.P.'s
Teachers
Students
Lab Rats/Dissection Frogs
Substitute Teachers

Called to the Principals Office
Tuesday 3/22/20
Year Books and Hawaiian Shirts

During my prep period Tuesday, I receive an e-mail form the Principal asking me to stop by his office Wednesday morning.

Wednesday morning I walk into Principal Dooley's office and sit in a plastic seat in front of the Principal's desk. He is tall, skinny, and a marathon runner. He has a dry sense of humor and could be a great poker player with the straight face he always keeps; an even keel of voice, always professional, never rising or lowering, and never yelling. He is also wearing a mask because it is the time of the Covid pandemic.

I sit down and ask, "What can I do for you sir?"
The year book picture. Why did you not wear a Hawaiian shirt?

"Your are joking sir?"
No.

"You are asking why I did not wear a Hawaiian shirt for the high school yearbook picture?"
Yes.

"It was my understanding that we had a choice to wear the shirt or not. Since I consider myself to be a professional, I like to wear dress pants, and oxford shirt and tie every day."

I appreciate that Mr. Geist, but I am afraid some of the teachers may think you are a prima donna. You see, every teacher wore the Hawaiian shirt, and since you are in the center of the teacher pictures, it looks like you are being defiant.

"I see. So when you hired me, I did say I was a team player, so if you want me to re-take a picture wearing a Hawaiian shirt, I will do so. While I think the idea is silly, for the sake of the easily offended, I will do so."

I could make a stand; but I choose peace over being right. I meet with the year book editor, and she photoshops a Hawaiian shirt over my oxford shirt and tie.

Who gets called to the Principal's office over a Hawaiian shirt?

"Pono" in Hawaiian is righteousness.
    "Pau" in Hawaiian means "it is done."

Boss Geist Post Observation Meeting with Teacher Geist: 2/16/22 in the Principal's Office

It is always difficult transitioning into a new school district, learning the systems and technology of a new school. I understand for the first three months at Innovation High School, when you got home from work, and after dinner, you often worked from 6pm until 9pm to make sure lessons were written for your classes the next day.

Thank you for taking your job seriously. for dressing up, wearing a tie daily and acting as a professional. Thanks for being one of the first people in your building (7:01 a.m.-7:30 a.m.) daily, after your 1.5 hour commute from northern NJ.

Thank you for organizing the 23 desks, cleaning them daily, in the time of Covid 19, to help keep the room sanitized for the health of your fellow teachers and students.

It is a stressful thing to get a new schedule, to learn the names of 125 students, to learn how to use Infinite Campus, Google Classroom and the New Boards in the classrooms, in addition to finding the best way to commute to a new job.

Thank you for cleaning out the clutter in room three, from the teacher desk and backroom full of boxes of magazines and school work from the previous room teacher. Thank you for making the room come alive by hanging 40 plus posters and 20 plus historical postcards.

Thank you for the 70 phone calls to parents you have made to hold students in getting them to hand in their classwork. Thank you for putting up your bulletin board with student work, a rubric and comments on each piece.

Thanks for having your lessons posted on Google Classroom daily and for getting your Progress Reports and Grade Reports handed in a prompt manner. It certainly takes time to plan, organize and write lessons, especially when they incorporate slide shows and historically appropriate videos.

I am aware you had to sign into the College Board to teach Pre-AP World History, and had to audit classes via the computer, before you were allowed to enter the site and to be able to post the work from their web-site.

Thank you for showing up every day for the students, consistency is an important part of the success of our students. It shows you are reliable and care. Thank you for taking your student attendance 4-5 times a day to keep track of our students.

Thanks that you have incorporated alternate (differentiated work) to help improve your passing rate by 21% from the Progress Report to the end of second marking period.

Thanks for attending your grade level and Social Studies Department meetings, being present, and giving suggestions and asking questions for clarification of best practices. Thank you also for completing all of your Vector Training video seminars in a timely manner.

Thank you for expressing to your Principal, Assistant Principal and Department Head, that you are more than willing to adapt teaching style to the wishes of your bosses to maximize student learning.

Thanks for purchasing a dozen games for the board games club you run on Tuesdays and Wedsdays. Thanks for your willingness to take coverages when emergency coverages are needed for absent teachers.

Thank you for going to the teaching coach and department head when you have had questions on best practices when it comes to teaching U.S. History, Black History and Pre-AP World History.

Because you are a professional, I know you will from here on in,

1) **Incorporate the suggested lessons, pacing, links & videos from the Black History curriculum into your lessons.**

2) **Create student centered lessons.**

   Thanks for being a team player. We value your teaching experience, and your willingness to adapt to best practices for our Jersey City students.

   In hindsight, perhaps we could have given you sample lessons as to what our expectations are for student centered teaching, but we cannot change the past; we can only move forward this day.

   I am here to support you in becoming a successful member of our team!

WORKING PERSON'S DILEMMA

I was complaining
to an old timer about work and he said,
"I do what I don't want to do,
so I can do what I want to do."
This is life for the working person.

One day a Zombie is roaming in my yard
and I wrestle him into my shed.
I asked,
"How is it being a zombie?"

The pale dead man said,
*"I do what I want to do,
so I can do what I do not want to."*

I asked him to explain.

*I love to kill and eat brains.
It is something I enjoy doing
but I don't enjoy
hanging out with acquaintances,
neighbors, family or friends,
because I have an insatiable desire
to kill and eat human flesh.*

*I enjoy eating human flesh,
but I roam, and roam and roam,
trying to fill a hole which will never be satisfied;
something I don't enjoy,
until someone cuts off my head.*

I guess we all have our struggles.
I liked Mr. Zombie and felt for him,
so I cut off his head.

Chapter 8

Guns, Terrorism, Covid & P.T.S.D.

SUB TEACHER ROLL CALL
HIGH SCHOOL IN NEWARK

DeShawn	Deja	Andre
Jazmin	Tyrone	Jada
Princess	Asia	Hakim
Demetrius	Marquis	Raven
Aalyah	Jayla	Jamal
Reginald	Darnell	Nia
Jaylen	Kiara	Willis
Essence	Trevon	Lexi
Miles	Imani	Hakim
Ebony	Imani	Hakim

Prank Names #6

Anna Graham

Chris P. Nugget

Dinah Sore

Eve Ning

Herb E. Side

Kerry O'Seen

Sara Tonin

Phil McCrackin

Travis Tay

Walter Mellon

PARTY LIKE ITS 1999!
1982

I was aged 16 when Prince's song "Party Like Its 1999," came out in 1982. In 1982 I was a high school sophomore and 1999 was 17 years away. In 1999, I would be 31 years old. That seemed like lifetimes away.

What would I be doing in 1999? I figured I would have finished college and grad school and been a pastor at a Christian and Missionary Alliance Church of 75 people somewhere in central Pennsylvania where I would go hunting and fishing. I would be married and have 2-3 kids as well.

In October of 1999 I began the career of being a high school history teacher in NYC. I had served as a minister from 1993 through 1999. I am married but have no kids. My 1982 prediction was only off by one state and three kids.

1999 comes and goes, and apparently Prince must have thought the world was going to end in the year 2,000. It did not. However, in 2016, Prince did die, and it came 17 years after 1999. Prince died at age 57 and was reported he to play 157 instruments. I can play the kazoo and the radio – making two for me.

In 2016, I am aged 51. Time flies. I am going to party like every day is my last day. I just hope I can collect Social Security for at least seven years or longer.

METS Charter School in Jersey City is Closing

Oh no, my school is closing!
Next year, here am I going?
Where are you going?
Students are lurching and searching.

Should I go here
or there,
or anywhere?

The end is coming;
The end is coming…
The end is here,
Snyder I will go.

Wishing and hoping for the best.
Where I go is the mess
where I must rest.

Annonymous
8th Grade

Newark Teachers Union Letter

February 5, 2020

Dear N.T.U. President,

Based on the articles I read in the morning papers, the Newark Teachers Union supported the Newark School Superintendent's proposal of closing four charter schools in Newark. I understand why public schools and unions would be against charter schools with no union affiliation.

Any argument that is controversial, is controversial because it has good arguments on both sides. I work at, METS Charter School (Jersey City Campus), <u>that does have union representation</u> via the *New Jersey Education Association.*

<u>Unions are part of the solution of improving charter schools.</u> **Solidarity means showing support for your fellow union brother and sisters, especially in the pedagogical field.**

The next time you choose to close down a charter school in Newark, the union should focus on the schools without union representation. *This is not Solidarity! This is throwing your fellow union brothers and sisters under the bus. It is called "eating your own."*

When a union lose one member, it loses power. I am sorely disappointed and betrayed by the leadership of the Newark Teachers Union.

Jim Geist
Jim Geist
Mets Charter School   cc: NJEA President

Jersey City Lockdown 12/10/2020

I begin working at METs Charter School – Jersey City Campus – in mid-September of 2019.

My commute to work is one hour but two hours home in bumper to bumper traffic. In the morning I drive around looking for a parking spot with alternative street parking. I witness stray cats, raccoons, and skunks walking the streets of a city next to the Hudson River across from the Manhattan skyline.

As I stroll to school, I pass the corner where two workers sitting in their van smoke their daily chronic jay bone. While I do not partake, I enjoy the smell.

I pass joggers, the corner bodega, the home with glazed green clay pots on the stairwell, the Jeep with the "Wander Forever" sticker on the back window and the white cat who greets me two to three times a week when I say, "Good morning puss, puss."

On the morning of clear skies and a full moon, our school will have a "Lock Down" announced at 2:30pm.

Since the Columbine High School Shooting in 1999, part of the monthly school schedules have been practicing "Lock Downs," where doors are locked, and no one is allowed out of the classroom or into the schools until the "all clear" has been announced.

The practice drills usually last 3-4 minutes, but on January 10th of 2019, no "all clear" s announced.

Students begin getting antsy at 2:55pm, since dismissal takes place at 2:57pm. The "all clear is not announced at 2:57pm, or 3:30pm, or 4pm, and students want to leave. I go on the computer and see the school has posted the following warning: "The Jersey City police calling for a lockdown of all Jersey City schools until further notice."

By 5:30pm, the internet has articles posted by all the local television stations that there has been a gun fight for several hours in downtown Jersey City. At 5:55pm, it is announced one police officer, two store owners a store customer and the shooter couple have been shot and killed.

The killers turn out to be Black Hebrews who do not like Hebrews who are not Black Hebrews; it is deemed a "hate crime."

The class becomes quiet after learning the news. At 6pm, the students are dismissed.

Not all lockdowns are for practice. I think, if this had to happen, I wish it had been on a Professional Development Day, because those meetings are
B-O-R-I-N-G.

POURING SALT IN THE WOUND

Depression hurts body, soul and mind.

Sitting in class,

A loud class,

Chinning up and white knuckling the period.

My insurance will not pay for my medication prescribed by my doctor. A smart aleck student says, "What is wrong with you? Why do you look so depressed? What is so difficult in your life for YOU to be depressed.?

I say, "Because I have so many dumb-ass students like you I have to work with every day," in my mind of course, otherwise I could be fired and lose my income.

I look at the student and say, "What if I am depressed? Is that the appropriate thing to say to a fellow human being? Do you make fun of a person in a wheelchair because they do not have enough will to walk?"

The kid in the du-rag (silky) says "You go no reason to be depressed. Your sad-ass puss is depressing me. If you hate your job so much, get another job!"

I say, "Does your face hurt? When I look at your face, it sure hurts me," in my mind of course. If I really said it, I would be in a meeting with Human Resources from 2-3 p.m.

Not only am I suffering physical and emotionally, this kid is making my pain public.

No wonder why so many teachers are booz-a-holics.

FRIDAY THE 13th 5/13/21
Retaliation over questioning my step level of pay?

I am not superstitious.

Life if good. I love my job. I enjoy putting lessons together. I learn something new every week about Black History, U.S. History and World History. I would much rather be paid for learning and teaching, than house painting.

I am working for the Jersey City Board of Education, and based on the teacher contract, I am being shorted approximately $14,000. Over a three month period of e-mails, phone calls, letters and the Jersey City Education Association making calls for me, I hear nothing.

"Things move slow in the Board of Education," I am told.

On Thursday May 12th, I file a complaint with the New Jersey Department of Labor about being shorted on my pay. I e-mail human resources and write, "If we can get this resolved in the next five days, based on the evidence I have sent you, I will withdraw the complaint."

The next morning, Friday the 13th, I have an e-mail from Human Resources. HALLELUYAH! I am expecting an e-mail that says, "Sorry for the delay, but we are in process of fixing your salary."

Instead, the letter states, "Your contract will not be renewed for the 2022-23 year."

Is this retaliatory? More importantly, can I prove it was retaliatory? Honestly, I don't have the energy or hutzpah to gather evidence and file a grievance. If I am not wanted - I will move on. I want to work for bosses who appreciate me.

I called for a meeting with my bosses a month earlier, giving them two weeks worth of Unit Plans to make sure I was on point; teaching what I was suppose to be teaching, and using small group work and student teacher lessons. They were satisfied – or so they told me.

I am the Wooly Mammoth who has been hit with long wooden pole with a flint blade. I am the bull in the arena with banderillas (harpoons). I am the buffalo shot with arrows being pushed by horses to the cliffs.

As word gets out among fellow teachers, I get pity looks. Every day, the pity looks are stones, arrows and knives being jabbed in further and further until I am pushed over the cliff of the school into summer. I get summer pay and insurance until the end of August. The blade has not hit a main artery nor my heart, but if I do not get a new job, nor unemployment until I get a new job, then the matador blade will have been pushed between the shoulder blades into my heart giving the final blow.

My neighbor Richie often tells me, "You are a survivor! You have been since 2013, coming up with ways to pay the mortgage and keeping food on the table."

When an animal is ready to die, it stops eating. I got up this morning and ate a bowl of oatmeal with walnuts, bananas and syrup for breakfast. I guess I am not ready to die just yet.

THE IMPOSSIBLE TEACHER's EVALUATION RUBRIC

As a teacher in a new school, I must be observed at least 3 times for 20 minutes, even if I have 20 years of experience as a history teacher.

The rubric used for grading is called the Danielson Model, created by Charlotte Danielson. Who is Charlotte Danielson? I don't know, I don't care. To me, she is a person who just gave the gift of micromanaging the already difficult job of being a teacher. The rubric is made up of four major components with 8-10 sub-categories per component. That gives a boss 32-40 areas to screw with a teacher's life. That is a lot of rope leeway given to bosses to noose teachers.

Is the Danielson Model universal in all circumstances?

Teaching is hard job, and teachers are not treated as professionals should be treated. Some are organized, and teach well. Some are organized and do not teach well. Some are disorganized, and teach well. Some are disorganized, and do not teach well.

I am organized AND I am open to suggestions, professional development, observing other teachers, reading articles suggested by bosses. I think that is the best teacher, one humble enough to take advice. What does one do, when the boss gives you evaluations, but no suggestions for improving your pedagogy? When a teacher fails, that is often the sign of a failing manager. I found this to be the case in my last job. It was like having a spouse, that when you ask, "What are you feeling? What do you want?", and the spouse responds, "You should just know what I want." Sorry boss, I am not a mind reader.

It is commonly understood in the teaching profession, many who become bosses do so, because they can not teach, they have poor classroom management skills. So what gives the right of a person who cannot teach themselves out of a paper bag, the right to judge the teaching of others?

My guess is, in education administration union charter, is the statement, "We who failed as classroom teachers, have the right to unconsciously punish those 'who can' by observing, judging, and giving remedial actions to improve the pedagogy of others, the very pedagogy we ourselves could not carry out. You know, the same reason so many who grew up bullied become cops, to beat people with billy clubs, or even easier, to just shoot."

Am I saying Charolette Danielson is as Thomas Thistlewood, the cruel slaver of Jamaica, using cruel methods to control slaves? No, her rubric is more like the Nazi regime creating data for files to be saved by the state to follow a teacher the rest of his/her teaching career. This is quite unfair for the excellent teacher who has a boob of boss who is vindictive, or a psychopath.

My neighbor says, "They do not like us because we are not puppets. Puppets is what the bosses want."

When do teachers get to fill out Danielson evaluations on their bosses? Fair is fair. Of course, one of the advantages of being boss, is whenever a worker offers suggestions to the boss, the boss can respond "Are you a supervisor? Have you been to supervisor school as I have?"

Bosses have the right to manage - to manage well or poorly; either way is defined as "managing." This is what the courts generally back up. And when a worker

FINALLY retires, if they live long enough, they look back on their lives, and all the boss directives given to them and think, "All the s__t I had to eat and all the boots I had to lick to get here."

If only teachers unions had mafia-like hit squads to make the psychopaths bosses disappear. I wish teacher unions were "less professional," and more of the Jimmy Hoffa Teamsters stuff.

Normalcy

Pre-Covid (February, 2020)
Alarm clock, shower, donning of work clothes,
commute, work
dinner, mail & emails, correct homework,
Jeopardy, MsNBC, bedtime

Nookie 4 times a month
Crazytown "leadership"

I drink 4-5 cups of coffee a day

Novel Covid Pandemic (March of 2020)
I watch Pandemic movies - Contagian, Outbreak & 12
Monkeys
hoping to gain insights to survive our
Zombie apocalypse outbreak.
675,000 Americans died during the
Spanish Flu of 1917 you know.

I teach Zoom-online classes from home
until mid-June.
Lose my job the end of June.
Collect Unemployment for 14 month
Mortgage falls behind 12 months
Credit rating drops, drops, drops
Resumes and Interviews
Watching Tiger King, Lady in the Dale
and Queen's Gambit

Stress, sadness, depression, loneliness, fear, anger.
Social distancing, masks, no vaccine in sight.
Self-medicating with whiskey and water,
R.C. Cola & rum
I gain twenty pounds.

Post Covid with new job September of 2021.

Alarm clock, shower, donning of work clothes,
commute, work, dinner
mail & emails, correct homework, Jeopardy,
MsNBC, bedtime

Nookie 4 times a month

If Hillary had been President in 2020,
we would have avoided hundreds of thousands
of needless pandemic deaths
under COMPETENT
federal coordination
& leadership.

Normalcy is boring.

Boring is exciting in 2021.

I drink 4-5 cups of coffee a day

Coffee is never boring
-pre or post normal

I Be Vaccinated...

Covid #1: 4/22/21
Covid #2: 5/20/21
Booster: 11/22/21

With the Covid vaccine, my arm felt sore, and my body, especially my back, feels achy the next day.

Shingles Vaccination #1: 2/25/22
I woke up at 2 a.m. in the morning with the chills. I could not sleep, so I went downstairs, turned on the television, and covered myself in two blankets for two hours. I began to get sleepy, and went back to bed.

For four days, I had a chronic cough, and had trouble keeping my lungs clear of phlegm. I feel sick, and wonder if I am suffering from Covid. I had to get a second Shingles shot in a month.

Shingles Vaccination #2: 3/4/22
I feel achy, tired and grumpy for one day.

A buddy of mine, a N.J. fireman, tells me the most painful experience of his life was suffering from the shingles. He strongly suggests, "Get the Shingles Vaccine!"

I took his advice.

2020 Covid-19 Blues (lyrics)

James Curtis Geist - Hewitt N.J.

It was February of 2020,
When the President boasted
"You have nothing to fear
of Bat Soup Flu curry.
Go to school, keep on shopping
This virus will soon disappear -
supreme is keeping the economy popping."

He wore no mask,
made fun of those who did
"Covid is a hoax, it will disappear"
381 K dead by end of year.
Spanish Flu killing one thousand x 675
Will 1918 teach us how to survive?

Chef Typhoid Mary's unwashed hands
spread typhoid through cooking pans
the "Patriots" ignoring quarantine
cock-walking at Super Spreader scenes
Going to church, bars, ma and pas'
the Virus spread its uncivilized claws.

It killed the rich, it killed the poor
It killed believers, atheists and more
It killed the young, it killed the old
It killed the Dems and G of P.
The Cult more concerned over a
quarterback protest on bent knee.

Hospitals & Nursing homes begged
for Personal Protective Equipment
Losing nurse lives saving life resentment
For Governors not loyal to the Don
ventilators, masks and gowns
withheld by President Genghis Khan,

Don't call us heroes and not quarantine
When pro-hoaxers get non-hoax sick
Exposing nurse angels is the selfish gene.
Hospital workers reliable and full of empathy
only ask you follow safety protocol
Blue Angel Fly Overs only produces gall.

Vaccine approved December 2020
Operation Warp Speed created per plea
Three million to be injected a day
For the 80% mark in June-way
All the Covid Hoaxer Senators
first in line for the Vaccine spray.

It killed the rich, it killed the poor
It killed believers, atheists and more
It killed the young, it killed the old
It killed the Dems and G of P
The Cult more concerned over a
quarterback protest on bent knee

Bridge: <u>Waterbomb the Cathedral</u>
<u>Forest fire raking squall</u>
<u>Dropping nukes in hurricanes</u>
<u>Eclipse Staring by the Boar</u>
<u>Clorox injections are a Covid cure</u>
<u>It's Presidential Dereliction in Crazy Town</u>

Pandemic tombstones engraved:
    *went to the beach
    *went to football game
    *too poor to not work as a grocery clerk
    *ignored Zoom meetings and
        now in memorial frame.

It killed the rich, it killed the poor
It killed believers, atheists and more
It killed the young, it killed the old
It killed the Dems and G of P
The Cult more concerned over a
quarterback protest on bent knee.

Wear a seat belt, sunscreen and
bicycle and motorcycle helmet
wear your mask and wash your hands
unless you want to contribute to the
mortician, grave digger and florist brand.

COVID PANDEMIC MASKS
March 2022

In the 2021-22 School Year, and everyone wears a mask to the school - staff, students, teachers, visitors, et. al. I have to learn 125 student names, and can only identify them from mid-nose, half cheeks, eyes and hair.

I can remember Dr. Tite Tienou, when I attended the Alliance Theological Seminary (1990-93) asking our theology class, "Which part of the female body is the most beautiful?" I am a calf man – give me a woman with nice gams, and strong calves and I am pleased.

The class sits silently, to shy, to priestly to give any honest answers. Dr. Tienou says after a long silence, "The eyes, of course." It is true. Some people have amazing eyes! The masks really bring out the eyes.

What if a deaf student reads lips, what are they to do in this mass masked pandemic period? I purchase a mask that has a rectangular plastic, so you can see my lips and teeth when I speak. I wear it for one day. People are looking at me funny. I
look in the mirror, and IT IS DISTURBING. It must be no mask, or full mask!

On Monday March 7th, 2022 N.J. Governor Phil Murphy gives the okay to lift the mandatory mask wearing. I am taking the mask off! I am a science person. I have had the two vaccinations, and the booster. I may still be able to carry the virus, I may be able to catch the virus, but I am going to live.

As the "unmasking" takes place, I cannot even recognize some of my students. My brain must know connect the upper 50% of the face with the new 50% of the lower face I have never seen before.

Those who keep the masks on, cannot look me in the eye, like I can shoot Covid germs at them as Godzilla shoots rays of radiation from his mouth.

I have a flashback of the Three Stooges, dancing with a harem of female servants with stellar bodies, in their Middle Eastern clothes and masked veils, however, when the veils come off, they have moles, bad teeth and beards.

The 3/7/22 "un-masking," reveals it is better for some to keep the masks on.

American Doer Coverage

"My school was closed by the state of New Jersey, and my last pay check was June 30th and my health coverage ended August 30th."

"Can I please get my blood pressure and depression medication?"

"Are you 26 or younger covered by a parent's health insurance?"

"No."

"If you are 65, you get Medicare coverage. Are you 65 or older?"

"No."

"You have to be a doer."

"A what?"

"A doer - you know - work. Do, do, do-da-do at a workplace. You must work for a company that provides health insurance."

"I want to work, but I have not been re-hired yet."

"Well, until you start doing again, you cannot be covered."

"That is ridiculous; illogical!"

"I did not make the rules."

> *"I am having headaches, and sometimes get the chills because my blood pressure is through the roof. My depression is worse since I have no more prescriptions for my Viibryd. My hyper-tension is off the charts because I keep looking for work, have no insurance, I fear I could have a heart attack."*

"I am sorry to hear this, but at least half the leaders of our legislative branch, believe only doers between 27 through 64 should not have coverage, unless they are a doer - or married to doer. You must learn to live with pain. Chin up! Perhaps seeing a faith-healer at a revival meeting?"

> *If I get cancer, or in a auto accident, or have a heart attack, how do I get treatment without insurance?*

"You will get treatment, but you will have to pay out of pocket. If your family is not wealthy, you can pay with what little you have until your bank account is depleted, then you can sell your home to pay the rest off. After you go bankrupt, then Medicaid kicks in. Medicaid is aid for the poor. Medicare is care for the elderly."

> *???*

"There is a 38 year period of your existence, when you 'must do' to get health coverage."

> *"And when I get suicidal from the pain of headaches and untreated depression?"*

"Self-medication, St. John's Wort, and/or prayer!"

"Does a person, an American, have value for being?"

"In the Kingdom of God, yes! If a person is born a quadriplegic, or becomes one through a traumatic event, they would be able to get disability insurance. They get non-doing health insurance because they can no longer work."

> *"So, most of the politicians who attend evangelical churches, love God, and country, do not support universal health care for fellow Americans from age 27 to age 65?"*

"In the Republic of the supposedly Christian nation of the United States, no."

> *Are you aware, 31 of the 32 first world countries, have universal health coverage, whether you work or not?*

"For me, I would rather die a Jesus loving American that allows 17,000 Americans to die a year from lack of health coverage than a health care system that treats every American for less than what Americans pay for health care today, if it happens to be Socialist. "

> *"Doing is more important than being?"*

"In America, for at least 38 years, yes - if you want health coverage."

HOW WAS SCHOOL TODAY?

MONDAY:
Mother: Did you hear what happened at school today?
Father: What happened at school today?
Son: I was late to Science class, it was my third late, so I had to sit detention after school today.

Mother: NO! There was a school shooting today!
Father: What? Where you shot son?
Son: No.

Father: So why were you late to class?

TUESDAY:
Mother: Did you hear what happened at school today?
Father: No. What happened?
Son: I had to go to the nurse's office. I sprained my ankle in gym class.

Mother: NO! There was another school shooting!
Father: Were you shot son?
Son: No.

Father: So how did you sprain your ankle?

WEDNESDAY:
Mother: Did you hear what happened at school today?
Father: What happened?
Son: I got a D on my history test today.

Mother: NO! There was a school shooting today!

Father: Where you hit son?
Son: No.

Father: Well, at least you did not fail your test.

THURSDAY:
Mother: Did you hear what happened at school today?
Father: Hhhmmm? A school shooting?
Son: No. In my home economics class, Billy threw a pencil at me and it stuck in my temple.

Mother: NO! Someone set off a bomb in the locker room at school today!
Father: Son, where you hit with any shrapnel?
Son: No.

Father: So the pencil did not poke you in the eye?

FRIDAY:
Mother: Did you hear what happened at school today?
Father: Johnny was suspended?
Son: No.

Mother: Johnny was nicked by a ricocheted bullet today.
Father: Did the nurse clean the nick with rubbing alcohol and put a band-aid on it?
Son: Yes.

Father: I am just glad you were not suspended!

THE HOAX

Go to School. Follow the Rules.
Go the 1st to get to second, second to third and so forth
    until you graduate high school and
    then college and possibly Graduate School.

Go to work –make things. . .at some point it may
    feel like a grind. And **we teach our children**
    who teach their children who teach their children
    to survive.

Are you having fun? Are you surviving or living?

And you work hard **meeting your quotas**, and
    one day **you become Vice President** and you say,
    "I have arrived!"

And <u>when you retire and have wealth and leisure time</u>,
    you are also impotent, have false teeth and you
    are tired.

You look back and realize, life started out as a hoax,
    and turns out to be a hoax in the end. . . unless you
    learn to become an individual – to live beyond
    what the ego tells you to do.

Tap into your TRUE SELF while you live.

Let go of responsibility and let you inner child play.
    Act goofy sometimes.
        Try new things.
            Be Present. Live in the Now!
                PLAY!

My Negro Problem

In 1970, aged 5, at a family gathering, I heard Uncles complain about Puerto Rican moving into Allentown calling black people negroes, some using the n-word.

A few months later in the summer of 1971, I called a man negro under my breath, from the concrete stairwell of my Grandmother's porch across the street from a public park, but in reality, I used the n-word.

He heard me, and I could see the pain in his eyes - and I have never forgotten the man's look, and the shame I feel for having said such a painful word.

In 1974, when I was eight, I watched the Ms. Jane Pittman Story on television, about a fictional character who was young when slavery ended and alive in the 1960's in the age of segregation. When I witnessed chains, whips, lynching, and the pain of the n-word, which forever changed how I viewed people of color.

In Sunday school, I learned about how the Egyptians enslaved the Hebrews, and I thought, God hates slavery, so much, he used Moses to help the Hebrews to escape from bondage. I saw it in the "10 Commandments" movie, where white actors portrayed Egyptian Africans.

Malcolm X was killed in 1965, the year before I was born, and when I learned about him in my mid-teens, I thought, if I was black, I would want a prophet like him to speak for my people calling Anglos "white devils" before his pre-Mecca Haj conversion about different ethnicities.

My father was a member of the United Auto Workers. When I read the history of Walter Reuther, I learned the U.A.W. union supported the Civil Rights Movement with money and an office in Washington D.C. The U.A.W. also helped organize and pay for the "I have a dream" rally in Washington D.C. in 1963. I was proud connected to an organization fighting against racism in the U.S.

In August of 1978, aged 12, I visited Muhammad Ali's Deer Lake Training Camp to watch him work out before he re-took the world championship for a 3rd time beating Leon Spinks.

I went to the Seminary School to become a pastor. I pastored in NYC and spoke out against child labor, sweatshops, modern day slavery and genocide in Sudan.

I married a black woman, and on the honeymoon, she told me she was quitting her job. I told her I made the salary of a teacher, not that of a doctor or attorney or a plumber. She wanted me to give her money weekly. I divorced her.

I transitioned into teaching in the early 2,000's, and some of my NYC students would say, "I love Mr. Geist, he is my nigga." They told me, the n-word with a was good, and the n-word with -er was bad. Some of the brothers and sisters I knew from Church believed, "The n-word should never be used. Never – ever – ever."

"What's up man?" "How are you doing man?" You are the man!" Where did this man phrase come from? In the 1940's, black American jazz musicians, to combat being called "boy," began to address each other as "man."

When I taught in Newark in 2018, at least once a day, a student would proclaim, "You're racist!" It hurt every time – especially when you pour your sweat, blood, and tears into your lessons and the classroom to help students so they may lead lives of gainful employment and reasonable contentment.

Everyday I showed up to the classroom – wondering when I was going to be called the "r" word. I am not a racist but…

So many troubles when the Spanish and Portuguese introduced the Encomienda System to the New World in 1492.

I was not born black. I am glad I was not born black in the U.S.A. Had I been, I too, would probably have moved to France, as Josephine Baker and James Baldwin did, Americans not treated with equal energy - as they should have been.

Living in a country of unconscious and conscious white supremacy, most Anglos who claim to not be racist would probably become better recovering racists by joining the 12 step group "Racists Anonymous." Put myself on the top of the list as a recovering racist.

GIRLS SCHOOL OF THE BRONX INTERVIEW

I interview for a history position at the Global School of the Bronx in early 2021. I am intrigued. I have heard statistics that all boy schools and all girl schools often do better than co-ed schools, and I would like to work at such a school to see if this is true or not.

I pass the first interview, and I move to the second interview, and I am informed a week later, "We have found a candidate to fill our position." For the sake of clarity, I want to know if there is anything I could have done better in the interview.

The Dean of the School said, "It was the question if have you had experience working with the Latino community before." I thought it was a strange that this was the question that would tank my opportunity to work there.

I said, "At Park West High School, the student population was 50% black and 50% Dominican. At the High School of Health Careers and Sciences, the majority of students were Dominican, so yes, I have experience working with Latinos."

He said, "I found your answer to be offensive honestly." I call a fellow friend I taught with in Washington Heights, who happens to be Dominican, and she tells me, "There is nothing offensive about what you said."

When I read the NYC Report of the Global World School for the Bronx, it states in the report the population is 1% Asian, 2% White, 28% Black, 68% Latino and 1% other.

How is what I said different than an official report of the student population by the City of New York?

It turns out I cannot teach there anyway, since one of the job requirements is being bi-lingual. Perhaps they should have advertised that on NY School Jobs .com.

Under Pressure -P.T.S.D.

My buddy has gone through a heart-wrenching divorce. He did everything he could to reconcile the marriage, but the other had no interest. He goes to counseling and attends an anger management class. There are ten people in the class, and nine of them turn out to be teachers.

Ironically, he works as a substitute teacher in California, and shares how hard it is to work in the classroom as well.

According to Education World, teachers are angry from:
    Disrespect from students.
        Instructions not followed by students.
    Lack of control of the class.
        Dissatisfaction with administrators.
    Interference from parents.
        Frustration with technology.
    Lack of resources.
        Curriculum constraints.
    Pressure of academic evaluations.
        Not being treated as professionals.
    Low salaries for the work required.

Puberty is a challenging time in which young people may become more sensitive and easily upset. Hormonal changes affect mood and emotions.

Frederick Lenz says, "Often in the student's confusion, she or he directs anger at the teacher, blaming them for the pain they are experiencing, or for their own mistakes."

Many teachers suffer from Post Traumatic Stress Disorder today, and in my 20 years, <u>I have yet to sit in a professional development addressing P.T.S.D. in the teaching profession.</u>

"Everyone has a story that leads to misbehavior or defiance. Nine times out of ten, the story behind misbehavior won't make you angry, but break your heart."   -Annette Breaux

So much anger and frustration absorbed by teachers, they too can become the anger.

<u>Trauma is contagious</u>. God bless the mothers, fathers, therapists, nurses and teachers of the world. We need to talk about teacher trauma.

Computers Make Your Life Easier
James Curtis Geist
JCEA/NJEA member
History Teacher
April 20, 2022

When I started teaching in 1999, teachers turned in grades four times per school year, via scantron sheets with lead pencil circle markings.

Starting in the 2,000's, teachers began recording grades by in-putting information via Bill Gates machinery. I guess it is fine, until your computer crashes in the midst of your grading input and you lose all your "data," use profanity, and then have to go to Church for confession.

In the 2010's, someone made the decision, we need to have "progress reports." Teachers now have to record grades eight times a year – thanks to computers.

I used to be able to keep one lesson ahead of my classes. I was then informed I must turn in Unit Plans, doubling my work done on the computer.

In 2014, thanks to Governor Christie, New Jersey teachers must now fill out Student Objective Goals, fifteen percent of our teacher evaluation, where teachers roll the bones of their evaluations based on the children rising to our standards or not.

There is now more opportunity for a boss to harass or push out a teacher – thanks to the computer.

In 2015, I am now told, teachers will be using "Google Classroom." I must create my unit plan, my lessons, and also input the lesson now into "Google Classroom," - thanks to the computer.

I use to grade student work and hand it back to them. Today, students submit their work through Google Classroom. I have 125 students, three times a week, turning in work each class comes to a possible 1500 pieces of work I must peruse each month. Students can "re-submit" their work if they unhappy with their grade, making my life busier – thanks to the computer.

Thanks to Google Classroom, students also e-mail me. In addition to student work, I now get e-mails from administrators, parents and students – thanks to the computer.

Thanks to smart phones, students cannot read cursive writing, or read the time on the clock hanging on the classroom wall – thanks to their hand-held computers.

Thanks to the computer, I have less time to focus on curriculum planning, research, study and lesson writing. Busier is not easier. Whoever said, "Computers make your life easier," lied.

I BE PREJUDICED SOMETIMES

Prejudice Story #1
Driving to school, I pass through the Route 78 toll into Jersey City which takes me to the Bayview Bridge. At the stop sign, there is no one to the left and I being to cross the bridge.

There are two lanes, and I am in the right lane, but will need to get in the left lane to make a left at the stop light at the end of the bridge. As I am looking at the large full moon to the west, I move into the left lane. I am so tired, plus, no one was around at the three way stop sign and I don't see anything in the sideview mirror.

BEEEEEEPPPPP!!!! A horn blasts, and a black Cadillac S.U.V. speeds ahead of me and parks diagonally on the bridge so I cannot pass him. A black man with a beard, gets out of his vehicle, inspects his passenger side and looks at me. I am shaking – my hands are literally shaking.

Where did this guy come from??? He must have been driving like a demon to catch up to me so fast.

This time of morning in the Greenville section of Jersey City are crackheads, drug dealers, hookers and police cars with flashing lights every three blocks. On one morning, a crackhead is in the middle of the road, preaching to the row homes, trees, birds and stray cats with the fervor of a tent revivalist preacher. He is the St. Benedict of Jersey City.

This guy looks like a dealer. I think he is going to pull a handgun on me. I put my hands in the air as if to say, "That was on me. Sorry." He takes his index finger and points to his head and lips, "THINK!"

This guy may not have been a drug dealer. I feel guilty for thinking it. . Two days later, on my way to work, at the corner of Stegman St. and M.L.K. Blvd, by the Boost Phone Store, and I see the black Cadillac Escapade. A drug dealer runs up to the vehicle, and the bearded man hands him bags of drugs.

Oh, he is a drug dealer. A week later, as I am driving to work, I see the Black Escalade, on the opposite double yellow ling break of the Bayview Bridge, trying to pass another vehicle in the narrow lanes, driving up on him like a bat out of hell, and the other car beeps at him, and does not let him pass.

A drug dealer and a impatient and selfish driver.

Prejudice Story #2
Every morning I get my $1.07 coffee from McDonald's in Jersey City. On this morning, is a person who has beard, looks a bit shady and is wearing an Islamic skull cap. I think, this guy could be a terrorist.

After ordering my coffee, and waiting for it, this man walks up to me, bends over, picks up wallet and says, "This fell out of your pocket." As I leave the restaurant, he waves good-bey to me.

He was the nicest terrorist I ever met!

Sometimes prejudice is right 50% of the time.

Life Before Smart Phones

When did it happen? In 2014, is the first time I worked in a school where all students had laptops and smartphones. The first time I noticed a cell phone was a young lady was holding the phone above her face. What was she doing? The phone has a mirror?

I remember when cell phones came with cameras. My Dad and I use to laugh at the thought. Today, I put together a great lesson, including a video and slide show, to teach and entertain the youngsters, and twenty of twenty-five students will be staring into their smart phones or lap tops.

The addiction is strong - AND IT IS ADDICTION. The withdrawl of forcing the children to close the laptops and put the phone is always met with strong objection and the constance resistance will wear out instructors.

LIFE BEFORE CELL PHONES

1) Students looked at the teacher when she was teaching.

2) We jotted notes.

3) We visited libraries.

4) We read newspapers.

5) We used maps.

6) Drivers focused on the road.

7) There were cameras.

8) Dating was more difficult.

9) Prank phone calling was a thing.

10) We listened to music on music devices.

11) We kept our thoughts to ourselves.

12) We lived in the moment.

DYING EACH DAY

<u>How will I go?</u>
Stroke?
Aneurism?
Cancer?
Heart Attack?
Car Accident?
Drowning?
Lightning Strike?
Cow Trampling?
Hippo Attack?
Shark Bite?
Murder?
Suicide?
Peacefully in Rest?

The could make a show
about all the ways you
can die. No sense wasting
valuable time worrying
about "the demise."

Until my passing,
I die the death
from the bleeding
of 1,000 cuts-
the daily humiliations
my ego needs to
help me get out of
my false self.

The Happy Man

School Nurse Hank was always smiling. If you asked him how he was doing, with a great big syrupy smile would boom "Fantastic!" or "Wonderful!" or "The Best!" It was disconcerting to me to see someone so happy.

He was smiling when it was sunny, raining, warm or cold. He was smiling whether it was Monday, Friday or any day in between. Was School Nurse Hank that happy or covering his Carl Jungian shadow of a hidden sad life?

Perhaps Nurse Hank was a millionaire; or had the most beautiful, perfect and submissive girlfriend, or belonged to the "Shiny-Happy-People" cult. Perhaps he was a serial killer trying to throw the cops off his scent. Medical cannabis perhaps?

It was a strange day when I saw Nurse Hank not smiling. In fact, he looked depressed, scared and panicked. In that moment I knew School Nurse Hank belonged to the human race that trod, trod, trod in the face of difficulties, depression and desperation.

Neither School Nurse Hank nor the other teachers were smiling on that fateful Tuesday after receiving an e-mail from the Superintendent the evening before (2/5/20) stating the Education Department of New Jersey was closing down our school.

Many expressed "concern for the children," I said, "The children do not have to work about paying a mortgage."

In the end, all working people are only two paychecks away from the road to homelessness. While you can live in your home 6 months without paying the mortgage before the Sheriff shows up to kick you out of your home as it forecloses.

Can you spell "eviction?"

The only thing that made me happy that day was seeing Nurse Hank behaving the way a normal human should respond to devastating news.

A.A. Chips on the Tombstones
circa the Winter of 2014

As I looked at the Tombstones in the East Dorset Vermont Cemetery of William G. Wilson [1895-1971] and Lois B. Wilson [1891-1988], I notice approximately 100 plus "chips" or A.A. tokens on the tombstone of Bill W., and half a dozen on the tombstone of his wife Lois.

Bill W. is the founding member of Alcoholics Anonymous, and his wife Lois is known as the First Lady of Al-anon, a 12 step group for family and friends of alcoholics. While she was not an alcoholic, she is called the co-founder of A.A.

The placing of the sobriety chips on a tombstone is a sign of visitation and respect for the deceased. Sobriety chips are given out for the 1st, 2nd, 3rd, 6th and 9th months in your first year of sobriety. After that, sobriety tokens are given out for yearly anniversaries.

While I do not identify as an alcoholic, I am grateful for all the 12 step programs that have been birthed out of the A.A. program. It upset me there were so few coins on the tombstone of Lois.

I moved half of the coins from Bill's tombstone to hers. I said, "Lois, this is for all the distress and heart-ache Bill put you through before his recovery. Thank-you for all you done for me and for the recovering codependents of the world.

Corey Wise of the Central Park Five circa 1989

1,2,3,4,5,6,7,8,9,10,11,12,13,14,15,16,17,18,19,20,21,22,23,24,
25,26,27,28,29,30,31,32,33,34,35,36,37,38,39,40,41,42,43,44,
45,46,47,48,49,50,51,52,53,54,55,56,57,58,59,60,61,62,63,64,
65,66,67,68,69,70,71,72,73,74,75,76,77,78,79,80,81,82,83,84
,85,86,87,88,89,90,91,92,93,94,95,95,96,97,98,99,100,101,102,
103,104,105,106,107,108,109,110,111,112,113,114,115,116,
117,118,119,120,121,122,123,124,125,126,127,128,129,130,
131,132,133,134,135,136,137,138,139,140,141,142,143,144,
145,146,147,148,149,150,151,152,153,154,155,156,157,158,
159,160,161,162,163,164,165,166,167,168,169,170,171,172,
173,174,175,176,177,178,179,180,181,182,183,184,185,186,
187,188,189,190,191,192,193,194,195,196,197,198,199,200,
201,202,203,204,205,206,207,208,209,210,211,212,213,214,
215,216,217,218,219,220,221,222,223,224,225,226,227,228,
229,230,231,232,233,234,235,236,237,238,239,240,241,242,
243,244,245,246,247,248,249,250,251,252,253,254,255,256,
257,258,259,260,261,262,263,264,265,266,267,268,269,270,
271,272,273,274,275,276,277,278,279,280,281,282,283,284,
285,286,287,288,289,290,291,292,293,294,295,296,297,298,
299,300,301,302,303,304,305,306,307,308,309,310,311,312,
313,314,315,316,317,318,319,320,321,322,323,324,325,326,
327,328,329,330,331,332,333,334,335,336,337,338,339,340,
341,342,343,344,345,346,347,348,349,350,351,252,353,354,
355,356,357,358,359,360,361,362,363,364,365…

1,2,3,4,5,6,7,8,9,10,11,12,13,14,15,16,17,18,19,20,21,22,23,24,
25,26,27,28,29,30,31,32,33,34,35,36,37,38,39,40,41,42,43,44,
45,46,47,48,49,50,51,52,53,54,55,56,57,58,59,60,61,62,63,64,
65,66,67,68,69,70,71,72,73,74,75,76,77,78,79,80,81,82,83,84
,85,86,87,88,89,90,91,92,93,94,95,95,96,97,98,99,100,101,102,
103,104,105,106,107,108,109,110,111,112,113,114,115,116,
117,118,119,120,121,122,123,124,125,126,127,128,129,130,

131,132,133,134,135,136,137,138,139,140,141,142,143,144,
145,146,147,148,149,150,151,152,153,154,155,156,157,158,
159,160,161,162,163,164,165,166,167,168,169,170,171,172,
173,174,175,176,177,178,179,180,181,182,183,184,185,186,
187,188,189,190,191,192,193,194,195,196,197,198,199,200,
201,202,203,204,205,206,207,208,209,210,211,212,213,214,
215,216,217,218,219,220,221,222,223,224,225,226,227,228,
229,230,231,232,233,234,235,236,237,238,239,240,241,242,
243,244,245,246,247,248,249,250,251,252,253,254,255,256,
257,258,259,260,261,262,263,264,265,266,267,268,269,270,
271,272,273,274,275,276,277,278,279,280,281,282,283,284,
285,286,287,288,289,290,291,292,293,294,295,296,297,298,
299,300,301,302,303,304,305,306,307,308,309,310,311,312,
313,314,315,316,317,318,319,320,321,322,323,324,325,326,
327,328,329,330,331,332,333,334,335,336,337,338,339,340,
341,342,343,344,345,346,347,348,349,350,351,252,353,354,
355,356,357,358,359,360,361,362,363,364,365…

1,2,3,4,5,6,7,8,9,10,11,12,13,14,15,16,17,18,19,20,21,22,23,24,
25,26,27,28,29,30,31,32,33,34,35,36,37,38,39,40,41,42,43,44,
45,46,47,48,49,50,51,52,53,54,55,56,57,58,59,60,61,62,63,64,
65,66,67,68,69,70,71,72,73,74,75,76,77,78,79,80,81,82,83,84
,85,86,87,88,89,90,91,92,93,94,95,95,96,97,98,99,100,101,102,
103,104,105,106,107,108,109,110,111,112,113,114,115,116,
117,118,119,120,121,122,123,124,125,126,127,128,129,130,
131,132,133,134,135,136,137,138,139,140,141,142,143,144,
145,146,147,148,149,150,151,152,153,154,155,156,157,158,
159,160,161,162,163,164,165,166,167,168,169,170,171,172,
173,174,175,176,177,178,179,180,181,182,183,184,185,186,
187,188,189,190,191,192,193,194,195,196,197,198,199,200,
201,202,203,204,205,206,207,208,209,210,211,212,213,214,
215,216,217,218,219,220,221,222,223,224,225,226,227,228,
229,230,231,232,233,234,235,236,237,238,239,240,241,242,
243,244,245,246,247,248,249,250,251,252,253,254,255,256,

257,258,259,260,261,262,263,264,265,266,267,268,269,270,
271,272,273,274,275,276,277,278,279,280,281,282,283,284,
285,286,287,288,289,290,291,292,293,294,295,296,297,298,
299,300,301,302,303,304,305,306,307,308,309,310,311,312,
313,314,315,316,317,318,319,320,321,322,323,324,325,326,
327,328,329,330,331,332,333,334,335,336,337,338,339,340,
341,342,343,344,345,346,347,348,349,350,351,252,353,354,
355,356,357,358,359,360,361,362,363,364,365…

1,2,3,4,5,6,7,8,9,10,11,12,13,14,15,16,17,18,19,20,21,22,23,24,
25,26,27,28,29,30,31,32,33,34,35,36,37,38,39,40,41,42,43,44,
45,46,47,48,49,50,51,52,53,54,55,56,57,58,59,60,61,62,63,64,
65,66,67,68,69,70,71,72,73,74,75,76,77,78,79,80,81,82,83,84
,85,86,87,88,89,90,91,92,93,94,95,95,96,97,98,99,100,101,102,
103,104,105,106,107,108,109,110,111,112,113,114,115,116,
117,118,119,120,121,122,123,124,125,126,127,128,129,130,
131,132,133,134,135,136,137,138,139,140,141,142,143,144,
145,146,147,148,149,150,151,152,153,154,155,156,157,158,
159,160,161,162,163,164,165,166,167,168,169,170,171,172,
173,174,175,176,177,178,179,180,181,182,183,184,185,186,
187,188,189,190,191,192,193,194,195,196,197,198,199,200,
201,202,203,204,205,206,207,208,209,210,211,212,213,214,
215,216,217,218,219,220,221,222,223,224,225,226,227,228,
229,230,231,232,233,234,235,236,237,238,239,240,241,242,
243,244,245,246,247,248,249,250,251,252,253,254,255,256,
257,258,259,260,261,262,263,264,265,266,267,268,269,270,
271,272,273,274,275,276,277,278,279,280,281,282,283,284,
285,286,287,288,289,290,291,292,293,294,295,296,297,298,
299,300,301,302,303,304,305,306,307,308,309,310,311,312,
313,314,315,316,317,318,319,320,321,322,323,324,325,326,
327,328,329,330,331,332,333,334,335,336,337,338,339,340,
341,342,343,344,345,346,347,348,349,350,351,252,353,354,
355,356,357,358,359,360,361,362,363,364,365…

1,2,3,4,5,6,7,8,9,10,11,12,13,14,15,16,17,18,19,20,21,22,23,24,

25,26,27,28,29,30,31,32,33,34,35,36,37,38,39,40,41,42,43,44,
45,46,47,48,49,50,51,52,53,54,55,56,57,58,59,60,61,62,63,64,
65,66,67,68,69,70,71,72,73,74,75,76,77,78,79,80,81,82,83,84
,85,86,87,88,89,90,91,92,93,94,95,95,96,97,98,99,100,101,102,
103,104,105,106,107,108,109,110,111,112,113,114,115,116,
117,118,119,120,121,122,123,124,125,126,127,128,129,130,
131,132,133,134,135,136,137,138,139,140,141,142,143,144,
145,146,147,148,149,150,151,152,153,154,155,156,157,158,
159,160,161,162,163,164,165,166,167,168,169,170,171,172,
173,174,175,176,177,178,179,180,181,182,183,184,185,186,
187,188,189,190,191,192,193,194,195,196,197,198,199,200,
201,202,203,204,205,206,207,208,209,210,211,212,213,214,
215,216,217,218,219,220,221,222,223,224,225,226,227,228,
229,230,231,232,233,234,235,236,237,238,239,240,241,242,
243,244,245,246,247,248,249,250,251,252,253,254,255,256,
257,258,259,260,261,262,263,264,265,266,267,268,269,270,
271,272,273,274,275,276,277,278,279,280,281,282,283,284,
285,286,287,288,289,290,291,292,293,294,295,296,297,298,
299,300,301,302,303,304,305,306,307,308,309,310,311,312,
313,314,315,316,317,318,319,320,321,322,323,324,325,326,
327,328,329,330,331,332,333,334,335,336,337,338,339,340,
341,342,343,344,345,346,347,348,349,350,351,252,353,354,
355,356,357,358,359,360,361,362,363,364,365…

1,2,3,4,5,6,7,8,9,10,11,12,13,14,15,16,17,18,19,20,21,22,23,24,
25,26,27,28,29,30,31,32,33,34,35,36,37,38,39,40,41,42,43,44,
45,46,47,48,49,50,51,52,53,54,55,56,57,58,59,60,61,62,63,64,
65,66,67,68,69,70,71,72,73,74,75,76,77,78,79,80,81,82,83,84
,85,86,87,88,89,90,91,92,93,94,95,95,96,97,98,99,100,101,102,
103,104,105,106,107,108,109,110,111,112,113,114,115,116,
117,118,119,120,121,122,123,124,125,126,127,128,129,130,
131,132,133,134,135,136,137,138,139,140,141,142,143,144,
145,146,147,148,149,150,151,152,153,154,155,156,157,158,
159,160,161,162,163,164,165,166,167,168,169,170,171,172,

173,174,175,176,177,178,179,180,181,182,183,184,185,186,
187,188,189,190,191,192,193,194,195,196,197,198,199,200,
201,202,203,204,205,206,207,208,209,210,211,212,213,214,
215,216,217,218,219,220,221,222,223,224,225,226,227,228,
229,230,231,232,233,234,235,236,237,238,239,240,241,242,
243,244,245,246,247,248,249,250,251,252,253,254,255,256,
257,258,259,260,261,262,263,264,265,266,267,268,269,270,
271,272,273,274,275,276,277,278,279,280,281,282,283,284,
285,286,287,288,289,290,291,292,293,294,295,296,297,298,
299,300,301,302,303,304,305,306,307,308,309,310,311,312,
313,314,315,316,317,318,319,320,321,322,323,324,325,326,
327,328,329,330,331,332,333,334,335,336,337,338,339,340,
341,342,343,344,345,346,347,348,349,350,351,252,353,354,
355,356,357,358,359,360,361,362,363,364,365…

1,2,3,4,5,6,7,8,9,10,11,12,13,14,15,16,17,18,19,20,21,22,23,24,
25,26,27,28,29,30,31,32,33,34,35,36,37,38,39,40,41,42,43,44,
45,46,47,48,49,50,51,52,53,54,55,56,57,58,59,60,61,62,63,64,
65,66,67,68,69,70,71,72,73,74,75,76,77,78,79,80,81,82,83,84
,85,86,87,88,89,90,91,92,93,94,95,95,96,97,98,99,100,101,102,
103,104,105,106,107,108,109,110,111,112,113,114,115,116,
117,118,119,120,121,122,123,124,125,126,127,128,129,130,
131,132,133,134,135,136,137,138,139,140,141,142,143,144,
145,146,147,148,149,150,151,152,153,154,155,156,157,158,
159,160,161,162,163,164,165,166,167,168,169,170,171,172,
173,174,175,176,177,178,179,180,181,182,183,184,185,186,
187,188,189,190,191,192,193,194,195,196,197,198,199,200,
201,202,203,204,205,206,207,208,209,210,211,212,213,214,
215,216,217,218,219,220,221,222,223,224,225,226,227,228,
229,230,231,232,233,234,235,236,237,238,239,240,241,242,
243,244,245,246,247,248,249,250,251,252,253,254,255,256,
257,258,259,260,261,262,263,264,265,266,267,268,269,270,
271,272,273,274,275,276,277,278,279,280,281,282,283,284,
285,286,287,288,289,290,291,292,293,294,295,296,297,298,

299,300,301,302,303,304,305,306,307,308,309,310,311,312,
313,314,315,316,317,318,319,320,321,322,323,324,325,326,
327,328,329,330,331,332,333,334,335,336,337,338,339,340,
341,342,343,344,345,346,347,348,349,350,351,252,353,354,
355,356,357,358,359,360,361,362,363,364,365…

1,2,3,4,5,6,7,8,9,10,11,12,13,14,15,16,17,18,19,20,21,22,23,24,
25,26,27,28,29,30,31,32,33,34,35,36,37,38,39,40,41,42,43,44,
45,46,47,48,49,50,51,52,53,54,55,56,57,58,59,60,61,62,63,64,
65,66,67,68,69,70,71,72,73,74,75,76,77,78,79,80,81,82,83,84
,85,86,87,88,89,90,91,92,93,94,95,95,96,97,98,99,100,101,102,
103,104,105,106,107,108,109,110,111,112,113,114,115,116,
117,118,119,120,121,122,123,124,125,126,127,128,129,130,
131,132,133,134,135,136,137,138,139,140,141,142,143,144,
145,146,147,148,149,150,151,152,153,154,155,156,157,158,
159,160,161,162,163,164,165,166,167,168,169,170,171,172,
173,174,175,176,177,178,179,180,181,182,183,184,185,186,
187,188,189,190,191,192,193,194,195,196,197,198,199,200,
201,202,203,204,205,206,207,208,209,210,211,212,213,214,
215,216,217,218,219,220,221,222,223,224,225,226,227,228,
229,230,231,232,233,234,235,236,237,238,239,240,241,242,
243,244,245,246,247,248,249,250,251,252,253,254,255,256,
257,258,259,260,261,262,263,264,265,266,267,268,269,270,
271,272,273,274,275,276,277,278,279,280,281,282,283,284,
285,286,287,288,289,290,291,292,293,294,295,296,297,298,
299,300,301,302,303,304,305,306,307,308,309,310,311,312,
313,314,315,316,317,318,319,320,321,322,323,324,325,326,
327,328,329,330,331,332,333,334,335,336,337,338,339,340,
341,342,343,344,345,346,347,348,349,350,351,252,353,354,
355,356,357,358,359,360,361,362,363,364,365…

1,2,3,4,5,6,7,8,9,10,11,12,13,14,15,16,17,18,19,20,21,22,23,24,
25,26,27,28,29,30,31,32,33,34,35,36,37,38,39,40,41,42,43,44,
45,46,47,48,49,50,51,52,53,54,55,56,57,58,59,60,61,62,63,64,

65,66,67,68,69,70,71,72,73,74,75,76,77,78,79,80,81,82,83,84,85,86,87,88,89,90,91,92,93,94,95,95,96,97,98,99,100,101,102,103,104,105,106,107,108,109,110,111,112,113,114,115,116,117,118,119,120,121,122,123,124,125,126,127,128,129,130,131,132,133,134,135,136,137,138,139,140,141,142,143,144,145,146,147,148,149,150,151,152,153,154,155,156,157,158,159,160,161,162,163,164,165,166,167,168,169,170,171,172,173,174,175,176,177,178,179,180,181,182,183,184,185,186,187,188,189,190,191,192,193,194,195,196,197,198,199,200,201,202,203,204,205,206,207,208,209,210,211,212,213,214,215,216,217,218,219,220,221,222,223,224,225,226,227,228,229,230,231,232,233,234,235,236,237,238,239,240,241,242,243,244,245,246,247,248,249,250,251,252,253,254,255,256,257,258,259,260,261,262,263,264,265,266,267,268,269,270,271,272,273,274,275,276,277,278,279,280,281,282,283,284,285,286,287,288,289,290,291,292,293,294,295,296,297,298,299,300,301,302,303,304,305,306,307,308,309,310,311,312,313,314,315,316,317,318,319,320,321,322,323,324,325,326,327,328,329,330,331,332,333,334,335,336,337,338,339,340,341,342,343,344,345,346,347,348,349,350,351,252,353,354,355,356,357,358,359,360,361,362,363,364,365…

1,2,3,4,5,6,7,8,9,10,11,12,13,14,15,16,17,18,19,20,21,22,23,24,25,26,27,28,29,30,31,32,33,34,35,36,37,38,39,40,41,42,43,44,45,46,47,48,49,50,51,52,53,54,55,56,57,58,59,60,61,62,63,64,65,66,67,68,69,70,71,72,73,74,75,76,77,78,79,80,81,82,83,84,85,86,87,88,89,90,91,92,93,94,95,95,96,97,98,99,100,101,102,103,104,105,106,107,108,109,110,111,112,113,114,115,116,117,118,119,120,121,122,123,124,125,126,127,128,129,130,131,132,133,134,135,136,137,138,139,140,141,142,143,144,145,146,147,148,149,150,151,152,153,154,155,156,157,158,159,160,161,162,163,164,165,166,167,168,169,170,171,172,173,174,175,176,177,178,179,180,181,182,183,184,185,186,187,188,189,190,191,192,193,194,195,196,197,198,199,200,

201,202,203,204,205,206,207,208,209,210,211,212,213,214,
215,216,217,218,219,220,221,222,223,224,225,226,227,228,
229,230,231,232,233,234,235,236,237,238,239,240,241,242,
243,244,245,246,247,248,249,250,251,252,253,254,255,256,
257,258,259,260,261,262,263,264,265,266,267,268,269,270,
271,272,273,274,275,276,277,278,279,280,281,282,283,284,
285,286,287,288,289,290,291,292,293,294,295,296,297,298,
299,300,301,302,303,304,305,306,307,308,309,310,311,312,
313,314,315,316,317,318,319,320,321,322,323,324,325,326,
327,328,329,330,331,332,333,334,335,336,337,338,339,340,
341,342,343,344,345,346,347,348,349,350,351,252,353,354,
355,356,357,358,359,360,361,362,363,364,365…

1,2,3,4,5,6,7,8,9,10,11,12,13,14,15,16,17,18,19,20,21,22,23,24,
25,26,27,28,29,30,31,32,33,34,35,36,37,38,39,40,41,42,43,44,
45,46,47,48,49,50,51,52,53,54,55,56,57,58,59,60,61,62,63,64,
65,66,67,68,69,70,71,72,73,74,75,76,77,78,79,80,81,82,83,84
,85,86,87,88,89,90,91,92,93,94,95,95,96,97,98,99,100,101,102,
103,104,105,106,107,108,109,110,111,112,113,114,115,116,
117,118,119,120,121,122,123,124,125,126,127,128,129,130,
131,132,133,134,135,136,137,138,139,140,141,142,143,144,
145,146,147,148,149,150,151,152,153,154,155,156,157,158,
159,160,161,162,163,164,165,166,167,168,169,170,171,172,
173,174,175,176,177,178,179,180,181,182,183,184,185,186,
187,188,189,190,191,192,193,194,195,196,197,198,199,200,
201,202,203,204,205,206,207,208,209,210,211,212,213,214,
215,216,217,218,219,220,221,222,223,224,225,226,227,228,
229,230,231,232,233,234,235,236,237,238,239,240,241,242,
243,244,245,246,247,248,249,250,251,252,253,254,255,256,
257,258,259,260,261,262,263,264,265,266,267,268,269,270,
271,272,273,274,275,276,277,278,279,280,281,282,283,284,
285,286,287,288,289,290,291,292,293,294,295,296,297,298,
299,300,301,302,303,304,305,306,307,308,309,310,311,312,
313,314,315,316,317,318,319,320,321,322,323,324,325,326,

327,328,329,330,331,332,333,334,335,336,337,338,339,340,
341,342,343,344,345,346,347,348,349,350,351,252,353,354,
355,356,357,358,359,360,361,362,363,364,365…

1,2,3,4,5,6,7,8,9,10,11,12,13,14,15,16,17,18,19,20,21,22,23,24,
25,26,27,28,29,30,31,32,33,34,35,36,37,38,39,40,41,42,43,44,
45,46,47,48,49,50,51,52,53,54,55,56,57,58,59,60,61,62,63,64,
65,66,67,68,69,70,71,72,73,74,75,76,77,78,79,80,81,82,83,84
,85,86,87,88,89,90,91,92,93,94,95,95,96,97,98,99,100,101,102,
103,104,105,106,107,108,109,110,111,112,113,114,115,116,
117,118,119,120,121,122,123,124,125,126,127,128,129,130,
131,132,133,134,135,136,137,138,139,140,141,142,143,144,
145,146,147,148,149,150,151,152,153,154,155,156,157,158,
159,160,161,162,163,164,165,166,167,168,169,170,171,172,
173,174,175,176,177,178,179,180,181,182,183,184,185,186,
187,188,189,190,191,192,193,194,195,196,197,198,199,200,
201,202,203,204,205,206,207,208,209,210,211,212,213,214,
215,216,217,218,219,220,221,222,223,224,225,226,227,228,
229,230,231,232,233,234,235,236,237,238,239,240,241,242,
243,244,245,246,247,248,249,250,251,252,253,254,255,256,
257,258,259,260,261,262,263,264,265,266,267,268,269,270,
271,272,273,274,275,276,277,278,279,280,281,282,283,284,
285,286,287,288,289,290,291,292,293,294,295,296,297,298,
299,300,301,302,303,304,305,306,307,308,309,310,311,312,
313,314,315,316,317,318,319,320,321,322,323,324,325,326,
327,328,329,330,331,332,333,334,335,336,337,338,339,340,
341,342,343,344,345,346,347,348,349,350,351,252,353,354,
355,356,357,358,359,360,361,362,363,364,365…

1,2,3,4,5,6,7,8,9,10,11,12,13,14,15,16,17,18,19,20,21,22,23,24,
25,26,27,28,29,30,31,32,33,34,35,36,37,38,39,40,41,42,43,44,
45,46,47,48,49,50,51,52,53,54,55,56,57,58,59,60,61,62,63,64,
65,66,67,68,69,70,71,72,73,74,75,76,77,78,79,80,81,82,83,84
,85,86,87,88,89,90,91,92,93,94,95,95,96,97,98,99,100,101,102,

103,104,105,106,107,108,109,110,111,112,113,114,115,116,
117,118,119,120,121,122,123,124,125,126,127,128,129,130,
131,132,133,134,135,136,137,138,139,140,141,142,143,144,
145,146,147,148,149,150,151,152,153,154,155,156,157,158,
159,160,161,162,163,164,165,166,167,168,169,170,171,172,
173,174,175,176,177,178,179,180,181,182,183,184,185,186,
187,188,189,190,191,192,193,194,195,196,197,198,199,200,
201,202,203,204,205,206,207,208,209,210,211,212,213,214,
215,216,217,218,219,220,221,222,223,224,225,226,227,228,
229,230,231,232,233,234,235,236,237,238,239,240,241,242,
243,244,245,246,247,248,249,250,251,252,253,254,255,256,
257,258,259,260,261,262,263,264,265,266,267,268,269,270,
271,272,273,274,275,276,277,278,279,280,281,282,283,284,
285,286,287,288,289,290,291,292,293,294,295,296,297,298,
299,300,301,302,303,304,305,306,307,308,309,310,311,312,
313,314,315,316,317,318,319,320,321,322,323,324,325,326,
327,328,329,330,331,332,333,334,335,336,337,338,339,340,
341,342,343,344,345,346,347,348,349,350,351,252,353,354,
355,356,357,358,359,360,361,362,363,364,365…

1,2,3,4,5,6,7,8,9,10,11,12,13,14,15,16,17,18,19,20,21,22,23,24,
25,26,27,28,29,30,31,32,33,34,35,36,37,38,39,40,41,42,43,44,
45,46,47,48,49,50,51,52,53,54,55,56,57,58,59,60,61,62,63,64,
65,66,67,68,69,70,71,72,73,74,75,76,77,78,79,80,81,82,83,84
,85,86,87,88,89,90,91,92,93,94,95,95,96,97,98,99,100,101,102,
103,104,105,106,107,108,109,110,111,112,113,114,115,116,
117,118,119,120,121,122,123,124,125,126,127,128,129,130,
131,132,133,134,135,136,137,138,139,140,141,142,143,144,
145,146,147,148,149,150,151,152,153,154,155,156,157,158,
159,160,161,162,163,164,165,166,167,168,169,170,171,172,
173,174,175,176,177,178,179,180,181,182,183,184,185,186,
187,188,189,190,191,192,193,194,195,196,197,198,199,200,
201,202,203,204,205,206,207,208,209,210,211,212,213,214,
215,216,217,218,219,220,221,222,223,224,225,226,227,228,

229,230,231,232,233,234,235,236,237,238,239,240,241,242,
243,244,245,246,247,248,249,250,251,252,253,254,255,256,
257,258,259,260,261,262,263,264,265,266,267,268,269,270,
271,272,273,274,275,276,277,278,279,280,281,282,283,284,
285,286,287,288,289,290,291,292,293,294,295,296,297,298,
299,300,301,302,303,304,305,306,307,308,309,310,311,312,
313,314,315,316,317,318,319,320,321,322,323,324,325,326,
327,328,329,330,331,332,333,334,335,336,337,338,339,340,
341,342,343,344,345,346,347,348,349,350,351,252,353,354,
355,356,357,358,359,360,361,362,363,364,365…

1,2,3,4,5,6,7,8,9,10,11,12,13,14,15,16,17,18,19,20,21,22,23,24,
25,26,27,28,29,30,31,32,33,34,35,36,37,38,39,40,41,42,43,44,
45,46,47,48,49,50,51,52,53,54,55,56,57,58,59,60,61,62,63,64,
65,66,67,68,69,70,71,72,73,74,75,76,77,78,79,80,81,82,83,84
,85,86,87,88,89,90,91,92,93,94,95,95,96,97,98,99,100,101,102,
103,104,105,106,107,108,109,110,111,112,113,114,115,116,
117,118,119,120,121,122,123,124,125,126,127,128,129,130,
131,132,133,134,135,136,137,138,139,140,141,142,143,144,
145,146,147,148,149,150,151,152,153,154,155,156,157,158,
159,160,161,162,163,164,165,166,167,168,169,170,171,172,
173,174,175,176,177,178,179,180,181,182,183,184,185,186,
187,188,189,190,191,192,193,194,195,196,197,198,199,200,
201,202,203,204,205,206,207,208,209,210,211,212,213,214,
215,216,217,218,219,220,221,222,223,224,225,226,227,228,
229,230,231,232,233,234,235,236,237,238,239,240,241,242,
243,244,245,246,247,248,249,250,251,252,253,254,255,256,
257,258,259,260,261,262,263,264,265,266,267,268,269,270,
271,272,273,274,275,276,277,278,279,280,281,282,283,284,
285,286,287,288,289,290,291,292,293,294,295,296,297,298,
299,300,301,302,303,304,305,306,307,308,309,310,311,312,
313,314,315,316,317,318,319,320,321,322,323,324,325,326,
327,328,329,330,331,332,333,334,335,336,337,338,339,340,
341,342,343,344,345,346,347,348,349,350,351,252,353,354,
355,356,357,358,359,360,361,362,363,364,365…

5,110 days
of fourteen years
Corey Wise,
aged 16,
of the "The Central Park Five,"
spent in prison for
an alleged rape
in New York City,
that he
did not commit –

takes ten pages
to illustrate
the injustice.

How many of my
former special education students
are in prison for
losing their anger and
talking shit to cop?

Chapter 9

9/11/2001 @ Park West H.S.

50th St. & 10th Ave in Manhattan

The unsung heroes
of 9/11/01,
my brothers and sisters
of the
United Federation of Teachers.

"It took ten years to build the Twin Towers,
and ten seconds for them to fall."

-anonymous New Yorker

"The attack was intended to break our spirit It utterly failed. Our hearts are broken, but they continue to beat, and the spirit of our City has never been stronger."

-N.Y.C. Mayor Rudolf Giuliani

ATTACK ON AMERICA

On September 11th, 2001, 19 militants associated with the Islamic extremist group al Qaeda, hijacked four airplanes and carried out suicide attacks against targets in the United States.

Two of the planes were flown into the twin towers of the World Trade Center in New York City, a third plane hit the Pentagon just outside Washington D.C., and the fourth plane crashed in a field in Shanksville Pennsylvania.

Almost 3,000 people were killed during the 9/11 terrorist attacks, which triggered major U.S. initiatives to combat terrorism and defined the presidency of George W. Bush.

-www.history.com/September11

September 11, 2001
Long Island City, Queens N.Y.

6 a.m.: I stroll down my five apartment steps of 34-09 41st Street to the Steinway Subway stop in Long Island City Queens for my history teaching job at Park West High School (50th Street and 10th Avenue) in mid-town Manhattan. My neighborhood borders Astoria, Queens. I am donning an Oxford shirt, tie, dress pants, Rockford dress shoes complimented by my Land's End computer laptop bag full of lessons and corrected homework. I am after all, a "professional."

I love being a teacher! I love being a member of the United Federation of Teachers. I love my union representative Mr. Bob McCue. I love our union chapter!

Many of the Park West High School teachers go to Druids Bar on 10th Avenue and 50th Street, Fridays after 3 p.m., where school war stories are swapped. Students ask, "What do the teachers talk about at Druids?" Mr. Ron Nissman, the science teacher tells them, "We talk about students of course!"

For a new teacher such as myself, I get guidance and encouragement from elder teachers who may or may not be alcoholics. English teacher, Thomas Aquinas Shea, informs me one Friday evening bar side, I am no longer a young man, but actually "middle-aged."

6:05 a.m. I stop by the corner bodega and pick up

strawberry waffle cookies for my morning break. I run into neighborhood friends Jill and Jimmy. Jill has ginger hair as I do, and Jimmy has an athletic build. He works as a janitor in a building next to the World Trade Center buildings. In their strong Long Island accent they say hello and good-bye to me.

6:30 a.m. The New York City Mayoral Primary vote is today and I stop by the polls at 6:30 a.m. and cast my vote for Alan Hevesi. The election machines are in an elementary school gymnasium, next to the Kaufman-Astoria Studios where Sesame Street and the Cosby Show is filmed. After voting, I walk to the Steinway Subway stop on Steinway and 34th Avenue to catch the R Train.

7:01 a.m.: I take the R train to Times Square/42nd Street, and usually transfer to the uptown Number 1 train to 50th Street. On this day, I walk from 42nd Street to 50th street. It is a crisp and clear sky blue day. It is one of top summer days of 2001. I read the Daily News on my work commute.

7:30 a.m.: As the R train rolls into Times Square, I am full of anticipation that I am meeting one of my best friends, Dr. Ed Nanno, at the Bull and Bear Bar in the financial district of Manhattan for dinner. He works in Syracuse, with the Bank of New York and has a business meeting at the Deutsch Bank, next to the Twin Towers today. Ed and I were school mates at Nyack College (1984-88) and the Alliance Theological Seminary (1990-93).

7:50 a.m.: I am the Dean of the Culinary House as well as a history teacher. I teach classes for four periods, and serve as a dean for 2 periods. I clock into work, saunter into my office, turning on the radio listening to classic rock or Air America Radio, as I prepare myself for the school day. I listen to Marc Maron, Al Franken, Janine Garafalo and Randy Rhodes. The election of 2,000 between George Bush and Al Gore still sticks in the craw of half the country because the Supreme Court ended making a ruling that chose the President of the United States.

8:00 a.m.: During period 1, I work at student scanning with school security agents by the metal detectors checking for cell phones, knives or guns students may be concealing. We collect the cell phones, put them in manilla folders with the student name, and then give them back at the end of the school day. If a student has a box cutter, I have to fill out paper work for their three day suspension, and contact the parents and turn in the paperwork to Ms. Flo Jo, the unfriendly, difficult and crazed secretary for the Dean's Office.

**8:47 a.m.: *American Flight 11, crashes into floors 90 to 100 of WTC North Tower.*

9:00 a.m.: Hundred firefighters rush to the Tower and begin climbing the stairs to rescue people.

**9:02 a.m.: *United Flight 175 crashes into floors 78 to 87 of the WTC South Tower.*

9:27 a.m.: **N.Y.C. airports are shut down.**

9:32 a.m.: **All financial markets in the U.S. are closed.**

**9:41 a.m.: *American Flight 77 crashes into the Pentagon in Washington D.C.*

9:45 a.m.: The White House is evacuated.

9:48 a.m.: The U.S. Capital is evacuated.

9:50 a.m.: I walk the hallways to "encourage" hallway stragglers to get to class. As I walk up a stairwell, Mr. Wallach, the drama teacher, grabs my arm and says, "Mr. Geist, did you hear two planes have flown into the Twin Towers? There was a 20 minute difference! Also, the Pentagon has also been hit with a plane!"

WHAT? It sinks in; this is a terrorist attack. This is OUR generation's Pearl Harbor. How many have died? How many have been injured? I get an a sick feeling in my stomach, feel winded and light headed.

Each tower can hold 50,000 people. It is a number I remember from my Twin Tower Tour in 1986, because I grew up in Allentown Pennsylvania, a town of 100,000 people. The Towers could house my hometown.

9:55 a.m.: The Principal Frank Brancato makes an announcement calling the head of Security and all deans to his office immediately. I walk into his office, and he has the television on. Smoke is billowing out of both Towers. The secretaries screech as the news replays the image of the second plane flying into the second Tower with the fireball plume growing and rolling into the hemisphere.
The live television image keeps rolling as fire and smoke

billow out of glass craters created by the 747 jet planes as a lone helicopter flies around the buildings. In the 1993 WTC bombing, the helicopter could land on the roof. In 2001, the one building is covered in a dark smoke cloud, and on the other building has no civilians on the roof for rescue.

**10:00 a.m.: *United Flight 93 from Newark to San Francisco crashes in Shanksville Pennsylvania.*

10:15 a.m.: **The United Nations is evacuated.**

**10:28 a.m.: *Tower One, the north tower collapses.*

10:30 p.m.: The Principal tells the deans that he has placed security at every door to keep students from leaving the building. The deans are told to stay on alert, and that we may be pulled out of class to parole the hallways to keep the kids going to their classes. We are under attack, and not too far from the Empire State building and have no idea what is about to happen next.

Parents are starting to come to school to pick up their young people. At the pay phone, there is a line of 75 students who want to call their parents or guardian. For the rest of the school day, I sneak into my office as often as possible to catch the latest updates on the radio.

**10:50 a.m.: *The 110 story Tower Two, the south tower collapses.*

The unthinkable happens, and one of the Towers collapses,

like a controlled demolition collapse with a huge plume of dust and smoke moving looking like a desert storm moving through the streets of lower Manhattan. As the Tower begins to collapse, the Principal's secretary Nicole lets out a scream and another person wails "No, no, no!" Tears well up in my eyes.

The television images show workers, EMS workers, fire fighters and police officers covered in white toxic dust and civilians in shock walking the streets like the walking statues in a scene from the apocalypse amid collapsed steel, dust, and papers floating at Ground Zero. It becomes dark in lower Manhattan as the sun is blocked out by the dust, and human figures walk around the fallen towers as dark shadows. The steel girders sticking out of the ground look like three trident prongs coming out of hell. It looks like a nuclear winter has hit lower Manhattan.

News begins spreading throughout the student body. The kids will not really understand what is going on, until they see the horrific images on the television. I end up teaching my classes, really, briefing the students about the Towers, the Pentagon, the downed plane in Western Pennsylvania and reports of a bombing in the Capital Building and State Department. The bombings turned out to be false reporting in the fog and confusion of the terrorist attacks.

The deans, four of us, keep being called into the Principal's office approximately every 15 minutes for updates. The bridges and tunnels in Manhattan are closed. Some of the subways are not running. If you live outside of Manhattan, there is a possibility you may have to stay in Manhattan overnight. I really do not want to be stuck in Park West High School with hundreds of students.

11:00 a.m.: Mayor Giuliani tells people to stay home and orders lower Manhattan evacuated.

11:10 a.m.: The Principal makes an announcement over the speaker system informing the students our country is at war. At first, there is shock and silence, and by 1 p.m., the student anxiety and panic is building, and students began to leave classes and to head towards the exit doors. The staff had been informed by the Principal Brancato, to not use the phones. Half the phone lines are down anyway since much of it came through the Twin Tower communication antennas. Many television stations cannot be accessed as well.

Tears begin to fill eyes as teachers and students began to realize, they have family, neighbors and/or friends who work at the World Trade Center or in lower Manhattan. The teachers and administrators are waiting to hear from the N.Y.C. Chancellor as to what the next move is. The teachers, have worked without a contract for nine months. The hell with Mayor Giuliani's disregard for teachers, duty calls. Teachers are not teaching to become rich, but to help students, especially on this 9/11/01 day.

The UFT held a rally at City Hall for a new teachers contract and Guiliani had recently left his wife for another woman. His business really, but I made a placard that said, "Forget Rudy's infidelity, he is screwing 78,000 NYC teachers." I must have gotten 300 thumbs up that day.

2:00 p.m.: The announcement is made that students will be excused starting at 2:10 p.m. My students in room 419 say "Good-bye Mr. Geist." As they exit, I cannot help but think, *"When do you know it is the last time you will say good-bye to a person?"*

2:30 p.m. Faculty Conference: The teachers meet for a briefing. Principal Brancato says he will stay at the school if any students cannot get home. I offer my space at my apartment for any teachers who cannot get home. The UFT members and administration are one during this act of war.

3:00 p.m.: I stop by O'Doyle's Bar in midtown before trying to get on a train. Some of the trains are not running, and people in lower Manhattan are walking across the Brooklyn Bridge and all other NYC bridges to get to their homes.

A woman, who happens to be black, is sitting next to me and tells me, "I work at the Marriott Hotel next to the Towers. Tuesdays are my day off." As the patrons are watching the television to get the latest news, it hits me, *I hope Ed is okay. Please God, be with Ed!*

Father Mychal Judge is killed by a falling body as he administered last rites to a firefighter. His death certificate was the first from Ground Zero that bares

the number 1. It is said that many of the days heroes were just doing their jobs. A fireman says, "I think God wanted the Father to lead the people into heaven."

4:00 p.m.: The E Train is running, and I take the E Train back to Queens. Everyone on the train looks in shock. It is a quiet and somber ride home on the subway.

Every hour I try to get a hold of my parents and sister. It is difficult with so many phone lines out. The skies are quiet as I walk back to the apartment. I hear a jet fighter screech across the sky, and all I can think, with the hundreds of billions tax payers pay for the military is, *"Where the hell were the jet fighters this morning? Why were the shooting terrorist flying plane missiles not shot down?"* The fighter jets can be heard flying overhead every half-hour.

5:20 p.m.: 47 story Building #7 of the World Trade Center collapses.

6:00 p.m.: Mayor Giuliani tells New Yorkers to stay home Wednesday if at all possible.

7:00 p.m.: My sister Jody calls me via her cell phone and is relieved to find out if I am safe. I ask her to call Mom and Dad, and good friend Pastor Mike Brogna. I later find out Dad suffered a terrible head ache all day until he received word I was okay.

7:30 p.m.: I live on the third floor, and walk up to the roof of my building with a lounge chair, radio, can of beer and a cigar. I sit and face the Manhattan skyline where I can see the 59th Street Bridge, and the plume of smoke rising from Manhattan ten miles away. America will never be the same again after this terrorist attack.

8:15 p.m.: I call Ed's cell phone to see how he is doing, but get no response. I call his wife in Syracuse and ask if she has heard anything; she has not. I tell her when she hears from Ed, to call me as soon as possible.

8:30 p.m.: President Bush speaks to the nation. He asks for prayers for Tuesday's victims. Bush says "Thousands of lives were suddenly ended by evil. These acts shattered steel, but they cannot dent the steel of American resolve."

9:00 p.m.: The streets are quiet. At night, you can see the glimmer of the television screens in the hundreds of apartment windows. Neighbors are sitting on their apartment steps, swapping stories. I go downstairs to the front steps and light a candle. Strangers stop and talk. *These bastards must pay!* American flags appear all over the neighborhood and prayer candles flicker in the long night of mourning in an act of solidarity for the Republic.

9:57 p.m.: Mayor Giuliani announces N.Y.C. schools will be closed on Wednesday. Power is out on the West side of NYC and he tells us no more volunteers are needed at Ground Zero. Giuliani tells everyone to stay home at if possible for Wednesday, at 6 p.m., but waits until almost 10 p.m. to tell teachers to stay home. He loves the police and firefighters, but has such disregard for teachers of the

Big Apple.

10:30 p.m.: I fill up my bath tub with Mr. Bubbles and lie in the tub, covered in grape smelling bubble froth, and begin crying. I cannot stop thinking about all the lives lost, family members who have not heard from their loved ones who worked in or near the World Trade Center. I grieve thinking how messed up, unjust and cruel life can sometimes be. As a feelings stuffer, my feelings processing is usually only triggered by an emotional scene in a movie or by traumatic events.

In 1974, two movies came whose commercials on television traumatized me as an eight year old kid. One was *Earthquake* and the other was *The Towering Inferno*. The Towering Inferno was about a 138 story building where an electrical fire caused by faulty electrical wiring by contractors cutting corners. Firemen bring the fire under control, but when the electrical system fails, the elevators are deactivated. A helicopter rescue fails as it crashes into the roof setting it on fire. The building occupants, with the guidance of the fire fighters, use rope to rappel down the elevator shafts to safety. On September 11th, 2001, it was the Towering Infernos – plural.

It took ten years to build the Twin Towers of the World Trade Center, and ten seconds to knock them down.

I think about times I visited the Twin Towers. In the Fall of 1977 as a 7th grader at Raub Junior High School in Allentown Pennsylvania. Our Art Class took a trip to N.Y.C. On our school trip we visited the Twin Towers.

When I thought of N.Y.C., I thought of Mayor Ed Koch, traffic, crime, garbage and being mugged. I was a Phillies fan and hated the Yankees. I rooted for the Eagles, not the Jets or Giants. Movies such as "The Warriors" and "Escape from New York" clouded how I felt about New York City.

My buddy, Mike Brogna, lived by Hamilton Park, as I did, and we were team-mates on the same little league baseball and football teams. Mike and I were walking around one of the Towers and as we approached the elevators, and there stood Lance Kerwin, the young actor on the television series called, *James at Fifteen*! He saw that we recognized him, I am sure he was glad the doors closed before two giant fans could chase him down.

I loved visiting the museums in New York. I also was digging the fact that here we were at the Twin Towers, where the 1977 version of King Kong, with Jeff Bridges and Jessica Lange (ooh-la-la) were filmed. Here they were, the 110 story towers in life, that I had just recently witnessed on the big screen in King Kong.

The last time I would go to the top of the Towers on the viewing deck would be in summer of 1986, just before my Nyack College Alliance Youth Corps trip to Mali, in West Africa. Those six weeks in Mali helped me learn to appreciate the United States of America, such as good roads, hot showers, electricity, education and access to health care to name a few assets.

How ironic that the last place I ever wanted to live, became the place I would live at for almost eleven years (1993-2001).

Donald Trump's interview on WWOR on 9/11
Only a few hours after the Towers fall, Trump brags that his building at 40 Wall Street, is now the tallest building in downtown Manhattan. Actually, the 70 Pine Street building is 25 feet taller than Trumps building.

Wednesday September 12th, 2001
I wake up and go to the Big Apple Deli on Steinway Street to order my scrabbled egg with salt, pepper and ketchup on a roll with a NY Times, NY Post and Daily News under my arm. As I walked out of the apartment, two things stuck out. First, how quiet the streets and skies were. No airplanes are flying and I see no cars driving on the roads, unless it is a police car. It was so quiet, hand over my heart, I actually could hear crickets chirping on my street. I accustomed to hearing cars, the subway trains, airplanes, people talking, car alarms "alarming," music from radios and the occasional shouting matches of lovers or humans fighting over parking spaces.

Secondly, I smell smoke. I looked up and down the street trying to see if fire and/or smoke is spewing from an apartment window. It has the smell of an apartment fire that occurred two months earlier. It was not until the Big Apple Deli that the news people tell us the smoke from the 9/11 Twin Tower Fire could be seen and smelled from lower Manhattan all the way to end of Long Island. I gasp realizing I am breathing in death. There were police cruisers all over the place. As the day passes, more and more New Yorkers stroll the streets, since most had taken the day off from work, after the attack.

I feel antsy, like I need to do something, and write letters to President Bush, Senators Schumer and Hillary Clinton and Representative Joseph Crowley. President George W. Bush was upsetting me. He looks like a deer caught staring into the car headlights. I want a leader who was going to take charge. David Fromm says, "Bush looks like the hunted instead of the hunter."

2004: The 9/11 Bi-Partisan Congressional Commission
In the summer of 2004, the 9/11 Bi-Partisan Congressional Commission released its report. The overriding conclusion was that the government's principle failure in 9/11 was a failure to "connect the dots."

The C.I.A. keeps track of the bad actors overseas. The F.B.I. keeps track of the bad actors in the U.S. The **C.I.A.** had tracked terrorists moving internationally, but did not hand over this information to the **F.B.I.** once the terrorists entered the U.S.A.

The **State Department** was in charge of visas, but failed to catch the fact that several of the visas and passports of the hijackers were manipulated in a fraudulent manner.

The **Navy** had its own intelligence system and information linking the attacks on the Navy Ship Cole to one of the hijackers to al Qaeda was missed.

The **F.A.A.** had not updated no-fly-lists with the name of the name of terrorists. Passengers identified by the airlines own system were not checked and aircraft cockpit doors were not hardened.

2004: The Intelligence and Reform and Terrorism Prevention Act created the ODNI, or Office of the Director of National Intelligence which coordinates the FBI, CIA, and fourteen other agencies in the U.S. intelligence community.

2021: War in Afghanistan Ends

Soviets in Afghanistan (1979-1989)

<u>Background</u>: The U.S. via the C.I.A. under the code name Operation Cyclone supported the Mujahadeen in their fight to push the Soviet Union out of Afghanistan (1979-1989). The C.I.A. delivered thousands of tons of weaponry such as the anti-Soviet helicopter stinger missiles, the Soviets withdrew out of their country. It is estimated the U.S. spent 20 billion dollars over 10 years to do this.

Operation Enduring Freedom
War in Afghanistan (2001-2021)

Following the 9/11 attack, President George W. Bush demanded the Taliban turn over mastermind of the 9/11 attack, Osama bin Laden. Operation Enduring Freedom began in October of 2001.

May 2nd, 2011: President Obama announces the Assassination of Osama bin Laden. President Barack

Obama announces the U.S. military and CIA operatives located and killed Osama bin Laden, the al Qaeda leader, in a nighttime raid on a compound in Pakistan where he had been hiding. After the raid, the U.S. forces took bin Laden's body to Afghanistan to be identified and then buried it at sea within 24 hours according to Islamic tradition.

August 16th, 2021: President Joe Biden Gives Speech Ending the War in Afghanistan.

"We went to Afghanistan to get those who attacked us on September 11th, 2001. . .We did that. We severely degraded al Qaeda and we got bin Laden. . .

Our mission was never supposed to be nation building.

We conduct effective counterterrorism missions against terrorist groups in multiple countries where we don't have a permanent military presence.

I always promised to be straight with you. . . Afghanistan political leaders gave up and fled the country. The Afghan military collapsed, sometimes without trying to fight. . .We gave them the chance to determine their future. What we could not give them was the will to fight.

I am now the fourth American President to preside over this war (Bush, Obama, Trump, Biden). I will not pass this responsibility on to a fifth President.

I cannot and I will not ask our troops to fight endlessly in another country's civil war. . .Our leaders did that in Vietnam when I got here as a young man. I will not do it in Afghanistan.

My decision will be criticized. . . but it is the right decision for our people . . . And the right decision for America.

Many Afghan Women Feel Betrayed by the U.S.
Many Afghan women describe feelings of fear, anger and betrayal as the U.S. leaves and the Taliban take over. May women were able to listen to music, participate in sports, to get an education, and to pursue careers.

As I talk with my parents about the withdrawal of U.S. troops and what the Afghan women say, Dad says, "Then the Afghan woman need to berate their men, and tell them to take up arms against the Taliban. It is their problem if their Afghan men have no cojones and Afghan women do not scold their husband to fight! If the women do not speak up to their protectors to fight the enemy, the women are part of the problem as well!"

Quotes
"2 trillion dollars to train and equip the Afghan military over the past 20 years, and they fall in a week. It was NEVER about real training. It was about military contractors and corporations raking in giant profits. I am numb. I am sure everyone else who spent time in Afghanistan feels the same."
-Richard Ojeda
Retired U.S. Army Major

"Don't blame President Joe Biden for the fact that after 20 years of training the Afghan Defense Forces aren't capable of defending much of anything. After 20 years!"
-Joe Walsh
Former Republican Congressman

9/11 Anniversary
James Curtis Geist
9/11/21

Never forget.

I was in Manhattan on that day.
We will never forget "Never Forget."
How can those alive on 9/11/01 ever forget?
The images we have seen hundreds of times are
    etched forever in our collective gray matter.

Every anniversary, I live my best life.
I try to be kind to everyone,
    all have crosses to bear in life.

I try not to watch television those days.
I try not to re-watch the horror;
    but I do.

Younger generations must be taught
    the history, the stories and the lessons
    from 9/11/01.

9/11.
Never forget.
Confusion. Anger. Grief. Sadness.
Trauma brain grooves cannot be erased.
I wish I could forget.

Never Forget 9/11
James Curtis Geist
4/26/21

The "Never Forget" unity
of 9/11/01 discarded
in one generation by
M.A.G.A. propaganda and
the 1/6/21 "Stop the Steal"
Insurrection defiling and
sabotaging our Republic
for fascist patriots.

"Never Forget" *forgotten.*

The re-set button
of un-forgetting of
citizenship, civility and unity
in the United States of Amnesia –
seemingly only pushed
after revenge attacks
by foreign enemies
who shed civilian blood
on American soil –

Until the next
forgetting re-set button
is pressed.

Chapter 9

Sexual Harassment

SEXUAL HARRASSER AND HARASSEE

2017 has been the year of women coming out to "out" sexual harassers from their past. Enough is enough and kudos to those who have nothing to gain and everything to lose plus fear of possible retaliation from the "other."

There is a difference between sexual assault (4 degrees in NJ) and sexual harassment which normally takes place at work or in a school setting.

In 1987 as a sophomore in college, I passed a young lady I knew on my college campus and smacked her on the butt with my right hand and she laughed. On another occasion, on a college trip to somewhere, I smacked a woman who graduated from the college two years earlier and she turned around, got in my face and said "Don't EVER touch my butt again! You have no right to touch me!" She was black, loud, and assertive, and she taught me an important lesson.

It was the last time I smacked the buttocks of any person unless they gave me permission.

In 2013, singer Taylor Swift, 23 at the time, took a 53 year old DJ to court alleging he reached his hand up her skirt and squeezed her cheek. He sued her 3 million for costing his job, she sued him for $1 to prove she would not back down and because she wanted to take a stand for other women.

In 2006, I had the love of my life break up with me, leaving me for another, and I could not stop obsessing and suffering from heart break. She asked to break communication with her, and still called, e-mailed and stopped by her apartment unannounced in the Bronx, NEVER to cause her physical harm, but hoping as she stood on her 8th floor apartment porch I could win her back as actor John Cusack did in the 2002 movie "Say Anything," when he went to his ex-girlfriends with a boom box holding it over his head playing the "In Your Eyes," by Peter Gabriel. The truth is, by definition that legally is called "stalking," and had my ex not been such a decent person, had she filed with the police, she would have had a manila folder full of e-mails and a list of calls from me.

The truth is, if I really loved her, I would have shown it by respecting her boundaries, and hoping the new guy she chose over me, brought her happiness. It was my time to get out of business and to mind mine.

How do you know if someone wants to be with you? If a person likes you, they will let you know and keep hanging out with you. If they don't, have enough self-respect and self-love to let them go.

Similarities between sexual harassment and assault both are a) considered unwanted , uninvited sexual behaviors, b) personal violations that can result in harm, c) can occur in a single episode or over time with repeated incidents, d) often involve someone the victim knows and are e) often gender neutral.

In 2017, 42% of woman and 11% of men have been victims of sexual harassment. In the military (2012), those reporting unwanted sexual touch was 13, 900 men, and 12, 100 women.

I have been on the receiving end as well. On the Rockland Coach Bus along Route from Nyack to NYC, I had a bald man named Piaggio touch my leg with his pinky until I threated to have the bus driver call the police on him.

I had an ex hit me with a broom stick, and threaten to shoot me with my deer rifle.

I have had guys hit me in the testicles thinking it is funny, but there is nothing funny about the vagal reflex, actually it quite painful.

Twice in my life, gay men have propositioned me, and kept pushing after I said no.

An excellent tool for me is a document I found on the internet called WHAT IS SEXUAL HARASSMENT put out the Women's Watch at the United Nations.

Google www.UN.org/WomenWatch PDF

For me, I have not right to put my hands on anyone unless a) it is consensual and b) it is with a person I love. For my past transgressions, I make amends by respecting others boundaries and standing up for mine.

BREAKING POINT – Sexual Harassment

In mid-October 2017,
after one woman breaks her silence
that Hollywood Movie Maker
Harvey Weinstein has "sexually harassed"
her, and 82 others break anonymity
and say "me too!"

The "Mad Men" TV series
shows the "the boys will be boys"
corporate mentality where harassment
is the norm and a means for women
moving up the ladder to higher pay.

In a 12 step meeting, over seven
people share who they too were
sexually harassed by bosses.

I have never heard so many share
about such things – the national
conscience has been pricked,
and trauma scabs have been
scratched open stirring up
much grieving work for so many.

A friend who used to be in the
Screen Actors Guild shares how
Director James Toback hit on her
saying, "Meet me in the trailer
and I can get you a part in the movie."
She said, "No thanks, I already
have a job."

Another time during the shooting of Tootsie,
Dustin Hoffman asks CarlLa if she wants
a roll in the hay and she responds,
"Did you not just get married?"

Weinstein	(82)	Roger Ailes
Tobak	(200)	Bill O'Reilly
Bill Cosby	(41)	etc…etc….etc….

Say it ain't so Mark Halpern
and Senator Al Franken!?!?

Perhaps 2017 is the year when sexual
harassment will be taken seriously
in the United States.

Anita Hill testified in October of 1991,
26 years earlier in 1991 vetting of Supreme
Court nominee Clarence Thomas regarding
harassment of the sexual kind.

President Trump has been
accused of sexual harassment by
seventeen women, whom he calls liars.

We must define degrees and penalties
for acts considered harassment to assault,
and give the accused their day in court.

There will probably be no real
action taken by the present administration
until the departure of
"President P___y-Grabber

JoePa "Sanduskied!"

Growing up in eastern Pennsylvania,
Sundays belonged to the Eagles and God.
Fall Saturdays to Penn State Football.
Coach Joe Paterno, or JoePa,
was god, the winningest football
coach in the NCAA history
with 409 victories from 1966 to 2011.

Jerry Sandusky, Assistant Coach at PSU
for 32 years, is arraigned November 5th 2011
on 40 counts of misdemeanors and felonies
including child sexual abuse.
On November 9th 2011, Paterno announces
retirement the end of the 2011 season.
On January 22, 2012,
Paterno dies at the age of 85.

It is alleged Paterno was informed in 1976,
the early 1990's and 1998, and
evidence in contrast to the claims.
It is impossible for a dead man
to answer these questions in court.

Sandusky retires in 1999, but as a
"Emeritus status", still has access
to the college facilities.

In 2001, a coaching assistant witnessed
Sandusky molesting a boy in the showers.
The assistant informs Paterno,
Paterno reports incident to PSU administrators,

the administrators decide to not inform the police.
As a result of hiding the truth,
four more boys get sexually abused.

The Paterno family says there is no
evidence showing
Coach Paterno tried
to protect Sandusky.

Sandusky goes to jail,
PSU is banned from bowl games,
and given a 60 million dollar fine.
In 2012, the seven foot statue of
Coach Paterno is taken down
and hidden away off the PSU campus.

In January of 2015, the NCAA
Restores 111 of Paterno's wins
When PSU agrees to paying 60 million
to the 26 victims of Sandusky
and to the prevention and
treatment of child sexual abuse.

While much is written about Sandusky,
the child serial rapist, and
what Coach Paterno knew or
did not know,
this story is a tragic.

A dark cloud will always loom over
JoePa and PSU legacy.
It is a case where both reputations
were "Sanduskied."

What I find saddest is the lack of reporting
about the damage of sexual abuse,
and more importantly ways
of bringing healing to the survivors.
In Ireland, a person abused by a
Catholic Priest as a child writes,
"When you sexually abuse a child,
you murder his or her heart."

There is not a cure, but there is
a solution for those survivors of
of mental, emotional, physical or sexual abuse,
and it is called A.S.C.A.
Adult Survivors of Child Abuse
is a fellowship of men and women
who share their experience, strength
and hope to solve their
common problem of recovery
from the trauma of their abuse.

You can choose to let it consume you, or
you can confront it, and process the pain
to learn to let it go and live a life
of reasonable happiness.

At PSU, they say the sky blue and
white because God loves PSU.
Jesus said for those who
hurt children, "It would be
better for him to have a millstone
tied around his neck and he
be thrown into ocean depths."

Chapter 10

False Accusations Against Teachers

TEACHER DESRIPTIONS OF THE IMPACT OF FALSE ACCUSATIONS BY STUDENTS AND PARENTS

Dr. Elizabeth Mae de Leon of Hamline University
St. Paul Minnesota – Fall of 2017

www.digitalcommons.hamline.edu/hse_all/4329

summary by James C. Geist 11/25/22

*Teachers have the powerful responsibility of influencing students & supporting lifelong learning (70).

The teaching process is hard work. Teachers are in the arena each day trying to do their best. Teachers influence student lives and encourage lifelong learning (79).

As the nation's interest in schooling has grown, stakes for success and failure have gone up. Scores on standardized testing and rankings in the local and national media on desirability of districts measure the stakes of success. In this environment of fear of failure and high stress and emphasis on performance teachers have seen a rise of accusations brought by students or parents (71).

In Canada, 13% of teachers have been falsely accused. In the U.K., 20% of teachers have been falsely accused (7). In the U.S., enrollment for teaching programs in California are down 53%, down 20% in North Carolina and down sharply in New York and Texas as well (8).

Reasons for declining teacher candidates:
Budget cuts, student loans, and the use of teachers as scapegoats by policy makers (8).

What can districts do to help teachers who are faced with false accusations?

There is a need for conflict resolution training for administrators and teachers (73).

Listening well is the most powerful skill to bring to a difficult situation. . . For someone to make an apology, someone has to be listening (74).

Districts must work to encourage growth of community among teachers and administrators to form healthy emotionally supportive environments for everyone (75).

Suggestions:

1. Teachers should continue to form healthy communities of support with colleagues (76).

2. Teachers should build relationships with their union representatives (77).

3. Teachers must build self-care habits (professional & personal) (77).

Gone are the days of "sage on the stage" when the expectation for teaching was dispensing knowledge, providing childcare and the factory model (10).

Today teachers and students work collaboratively to create learning and meaning (6).

Cognitive theory says teachers must explain to students why they are doing what they are doing and how each activity will aid in learning. . . students may be less likely to charge the teacher is not teaching (77).

For administrators
1. Walking through a teacher through false accusations it is important to practice empathetic listening and offer teachers a voice (77).

2. Administrators must ask questions rather than approaching the accusations as facts.

3. The other implication is to apologize…as a simple way to bring closure to the situation and to move forward (78).

In Portland Oregon, Dan Domenigoni was the target of malicious complaints by students (2000). The L.A. Times reports he won a $70,000 lawsuit against student parents for defamation. He believes teachers should sue to send a message (3).

Even when teachers are proven "factually innocent," the damage has been done (13).

Considering the increased number of tasks teachers are being asked to perform and the high level of precision with which they must work, teaching is nearly an impossible job. Teachers must devote increased attention to more classroom details as well as to more time outside the classroom learning, planning and justifying their actions (22).

Teacher unions are nearly the only organization that has paid significant attend to the condition of teacher's work (25).

Where to get support for teachers: other teachers & the teacher union.

Some local teacher's unions have begun assembling lists of ways teachers can protect themselves from false accusations such as the Northwest Professional Educators page [www.nwpe.org] (29).

The Mayo Clinic reports from a teacher survey, many coping strategies for teachers are alcohol, prescription drugs, taking a day off, procrastinating, and exercise (33).

How teachers cope with accusations:
Processing with friends and family, prayer, meditation, therapy, self-talk, crying to release emotions, music and/or reading (51).

In the U.S. is a shortage of research on the rise of false accusations being brought against teachers by students and parents (19).

The over regulation of teacher work brings undesired changes such as job dissatisfaction, reduced commitment, burnout, loss of belief in oneself and an early exit of teaching (22).

Teachers are told to incorporate more and more technology in the classroom (38).

Teachers are more, not less likely to get fired than other workers, driving up the fear of losing one's job, income, insurance and disappointing others. No teacher has ever completed a school day with every item on their things to do list ticked off. It is nearly impossible (36).

The arena of teaching continues to change at a fast pace. . .these changes have resulted in the increase of teachers leaving the profession and a decrease in teachers entering the profession (39).

Teachers continuously report that the stress of their jobs makes it stressful to find time for family, friends, and relaxing activities. "I have not life other than teaching. I miss having a life" (35).

Innocence Project:
Wrongful Convictions

Exonerations in U.S. since 1989: 2,471
Total Years Lost in Prison: 21, 725
    Contributing Factors
    Perjury/**False Accusations: 58%**

The Innocence Network -iwcd.org

FAMOUS CASES OF WRONGFUL CONVICTIONS

1. Stephen Avery: circumstantial evidence sent him to prison, only to have it overturned with the materialization of new evidence.

2. Damien Echols, Jason Baldwin and Jessie Misskelley were convicted of murdering three eight year old boys. They were released in 2011 after a celebrity backed campaign resuscitated interest in the boys story.

3. Rubin "Hurricane" Carter was convicted of a triple murder and served two decades in prison before he was released in 1985 for criminally motivated decisions.

4. The famous case of the "Central Park Five," in which five fifteen year old black boys were convicted of raping a white female jogger on coerced police confessions were overturned when in 2002, Matais Reyes confessed to the crime with DNA evidence backing it up.

5. "A dingo took my baby!" In 1980, in Uluru Australis, near the famous rock, nine week old Azaria disappeared. The mother, for nine years, was believed to be the killer. Eventually, a coroner

found Azaria's death was "the result of being attacked
and taken by a dingo."

FAMOUS CASES THAT CAUSED HEATED DEBATES

John & Lorena Bobbitt
Did Casey Anthony kill her daughter?
The O.J. Simpson Trial

Security Guard Richard Jewel alerts police about a backpack in the Centennial Olympic Park bombing at the 1996 Summer Olympics. He is hailed as a hero until the F.B.I. consider him a suspect. He is cleared after 88 days of public scrutiny. In 2005, Eric Rudolf confesses and pleases guilty to the bombing.

The Fugitive (1993 film) Dr. Richard Kimble comes home to find his wife has been killed by a man with a prosthetic arm. The cops refuse to believe his story. Kimble escapes from the prison bus to hunt the real murderer in Chicago.

TIMELINE OF FALSE ACCUSTIONS and ITS IMPACT ON THE LIFE OF A TEACHER

9/20/22: Mr. Geist begins working at Middle School in Bergen County N.J. He holds a N.J. History License 7-12, but is hired to teach a 6th grade class.

On 10/19 or 10/20, I had five 11 year olds grld in my period five surround my desk and they were yelling at me. My period five, an honors class of 27 students, is my most challenging class. I cannot believe that Snooky, Bellatrix, Akasha, Ive and Hela are yelling at me. Image five 6th graders telling you how to teach and how to live your life.

I speak to an A.P., in front of two other teachers and a counselor saying, I need help with the "mean girls." The female A.P. says, "You know who is meaner than a mean girl Mr. Geist? Me!" I will talk with them."

As a result of this verbal assault, I make calls to 20 parents asking them to speak with their children. Classes become more manageable.

10/26/22: A mother of a child in period five emails me saying, "I know in your class is difficult. These girls are friends and I give you a lot of credit in dealing with them.

11/4/22: A parent stops by my room to talk with me because she is concerned about the amount of work I am giving the students. I speak with my A.P. and he says, "Mr. Geist, I look at your lessons every day. I like the rigor of your lessons!" When I tell the student she can stop by my room during my tutoring periods if she needs help, she says, "I'm good."

11/18/22 Meeting:

Mr. Geist called to meeting at 8:15 and that "his union representatives will be there."

Geist tells reps that some students are upset with the rigor of the lessons.

One person tells Geist, "Most of the teachers at our school are women. Our middle school kids are used to be coddled. Many of them do not want to be pushed academically. Also, you are a man and you are white."

At the meeting, I am asked why there are not books in class by the admin. I say, "I was told we use a digital book, so I do. If you want history books in class, tell me where I can get some."

I am informed several young ladies have made claims that "I stared at them, body-shamed them and touched them."

I put my face in my hands and say, "No, no no! I categorically deny this! I need my job and healthcare. I need to work nine more years to collect a pension from N.J. I have been a teacher over 20 years this charge has never come up. I have other teachers in class period 1, 2 and frequently in period 5 and 7. Ask them!"

I am told we will meet again, and with due process, I am to be given a chance to come up with a defense.

11/24/22 Defense Document Written

Point One

On the third day of class, in period one, a young lady dropped the eraser by the board. I bent over to pick it up for her, and she did the same, and our hands bumped.

Mona begins saying in a loud voice, "Teacher touched me! Teacher touched me! The teacher touched me!" In my 21 years of teaching, this has never happened to me before. It is upsetting and from day three on, I am forced to walk on egg shells.

Point Two
Part of being a teacher is practicing "area of proximity," which means to walk around the classroom to make sure students are on task and not playing video games on their lap tops. On one occasion, as I was checking the work of a student, Maleficent scolded me and said, "YOU ARE IN MY PERSONAL SPACE!" This happened a week later with another student, Wuornos, and I thought, "This has never happened to me before in my 21 years of teaching experience.

I am really walking on egg shells with these 6th graders!

Not in my defense, but what contributes to misbehavior
I believe part of the problem is there is no after school detention. There is no real consequences, in my opinion, on our students when they misbehave. There is a Saturday detention, but most detentions are called "lunch detention."

Lunch detention? That is not really a consequence. For many students, I think they see it as a badge of honor.

11/29/22 Meeting
With Admin and Union Reps.

I am told the following:
We will work with you on classroom management.
Read the school hand book.
Complete your GCN Tutorials (8 hrs. of videos)
Please don't use the term 'mean girls' anymore.

We want you to be successful! You can report to work tomorrow, Wednesday November 30th!

I say, "What about the false allegations?"

The admin looks at me and says, "What allegations What are you talking about?"

It is like being in a Twilight Zone episode. I say, "You know, I have been home for the last two weeks, sick of heart and mind, over the possibility of losing my job over false allegations made by several 6th graders? What is the consequence for them?"

The H.R. person says, "Mr. Geist, teaching is about attitude. Let me make the following comments:
    The students are our kids, nor your kids.
    We pay you to work.
    Do not come into class with a cloud over your head.
    Be excited about what you teach!"

I have no problem meeting with a teaching coach. I did read the handbook, and it is in their records because I signed – giving proof. I re-read it anyway. I also complete the GCN trainings by 11/30/22, as mandated by the state of New Jersey.

Cloud over my head? What if I suffer from depression? Will I be punished for having a disability? When it comes to body organs being diseased, why is brain disease the only one judged as a character flaw? Would you make fun of someone in wheelchair because they don't have the will to walk?

Do Not Teach with a Cloud Over Your Head
Wow. Do I disclose to my bosses that I suffer depression?

Under the Americans with Disabilities Act, an employer must provide accommodations for disabilities. I don't

really need any accommodations per se, but I just want my supervisors to be aware I may be having a day when I am feeling sad, depressed, or my body is aching from the physical pain of depression. I just don't want a disability giving me a low observation grading should I be having a bad day.

11/30/22: I disclose to H.R. I suffer depression

11/30/22 I take off of work on Wednesday 11/30. I am still reeling over what I have lived through the last two weeks. I have a head ache, a back ache and I still feel nauseas. I call the doctor's office to get an appointment for 12/1.

12/1/22 I call out on Thursday 12/1. I see my doctor for a physical and an EKG. I need to refill my prescriptions and the doctor recommends I see a cardiologist.

12/1/22: The A.P. who said she was meaner than mean girls, but told me I could no longer use the term "mean girls" sends me an email stating "we support you in your health which is why you have sick days." She goes on, "Let's turn the page and take advantage of a new start. . . your perception of false allegations have not been substantiated - I am unclear what these allegations are?"

I am back in the bad Twilight Zone episode.

How Did I Get By During this Time?
The way I took care of myself was first to write up my defense. As I was doing this, I took breaks by watching

re-runs of the Ed Sullivan Show, with bands from the 1960's, comedians and acrobatic acts. I also go behind my home, where there is 26 acres of woods, and I get a campfire going, and keep it stoking all day. As I gather wood on the hillside, I crank the radio with classic rock music. I also call friends to process what is going on and I attend 12 step meetings to share my thoughts and feelings, to get my angst out into the universe.

12/6/22: I disclose to my bosses I suffer depression.

12/1/22: I attend a professional development event – the NJ History Teachers Association Convention at Princeton University.

12/5 – 12/7/22: I am back in class, and loving it. On 12/7, I am giving a test, and at 11:20 a.m, during my free time, I say, "God, I am so grateful to be back in the classroom! Thank you for the administration supporting me."

12/7/22: Teacher Meeting with a Parent
We are meeting with Mona's father. It is two teachers, myself and the counselor. She is passing all classes, except mine. When you walk around the class talking with students and playing games on the lap top, it is tough to get work completed.

The meeting finishes, and as the teachers walk out, the father follows me in the swivel chair giving me the stink eye. I say, "It seems like you have more you want to talk about." He begins to make disparaging remarks to me, and the counselor says, "Let me get the Principal." She gets a security agent to stand in the doorway until the Principal shows up.

As I am sitting there, Mona's father says,

I know who your are. You harass kids.
I know who you are at home and in the classroom.
Does it feel good to make kids cry?
You are not so tough by yourself!
I bet you were bullied by as a child.
I be you act like King Tut at home.

I am sure you will lie in front of the boss to protect yourself.

Why don't you speak to me without your boss?
I answer, "I will not speak until there is a witness here."

12/8/22: I memorialize the event to inform the admin what was said to me. This father was slandering my character and acting in an intimidating way.

(2nd period): I have a student acting disrespectfully. The students are taking a test, and I go to the doorway and call the mother. She apologizes and thanks me for the call.

In the hallway is the H.R. person, and she is watching me like a hawk. The admin tells us to call parents, so she should be happy I am addressing classroom management issues.

12/8/22: I am called to a meeting at 11:30 am, and told my union reps will be there. I think, "What? Here we go again. I was hoping the admin would apologize for what the mean girls put me through, but instead, they acted like it never happened. I am expecting the admin to say at this meeting, "We are sorry for what Mona's father said to you. Let's talk about what we can do about this."

Instead the meeting was all about me. The admin said I

acted unprofessionally at the meeting with the father. They also said I put students in my classroom in danger by making a call in my doorway.

For 21 years, I have addressed students in the doorway to not embarrass them in front of the class, and now I am told this was an irresponsible thing to do.

They also claim I did not grade Mona's work in an expeditious manner the two weeks I was on admin leave. In my 21 years of teaching, I have never been late in turning in grades for progress reports and for marking periods 1,2,3 & 4.

They put me on administrative leave again. The union attorney calls me the next day to inform me, the admin is letting me go, and I will get paid for two months, until February 6th, 2023.

I write a response to the letter sent to me telling the bosses and H.R., "If I had run out of the room, tackled a gun shooter and stopped him from killing anyone, I would have been fired for leaving my room during a lock down."

At my first and second meetings with the administration, I felt supported by my union reps; however, in the last meeting, they sat there on their hands. They seemed more concerned about looking like "professionals," than being union reps.

My father and Uncle were U.A.W. representatives at Mack Trucks in Allentown Pennsylvania. Whether you were guilty or not, they gave you 100% representation. They would make arguments, they would yell, they would get on the table, they would point fingers, bang their fists on the desk and jump up and down. My reps sat there like they were part of the Queen Elizabeth's court, not even having the energy to say, "Fa, fa, fa!"

A friend of mine, who worked as an Assistant Principal said, "I had a teacher up for tenure. I supported him getting it. He worked harder than most teachers who had tenure. The rest of the admin team said, "He does not have the look we like to work in our school." Because this guy was not handsome and a man's man, he was let go. Mary said, "If the admin want to let you go, they will find a way."

The truth is, I was a teacher with no tenure at this school, so they could let me go without cause. I never had a chance.

Think of it, the student who was disrespectful, did not do her work, and told lies to the administration and father, had more power than a person with four years of college, three years of graduate school, 20 plus years as a teacher and 29 books under his belt.

Why are teachers leaving the profession today?

12/12/22 Termination Letter

One of the reasons stated for letting me go is that I did not complete the G.C.N. trainings by 11/30, but I did compete them by 11/30.

Why was this placed in the letter?

I am also informed via a Rice Notice there will be a Board of Education Meeting will review and discuss my current assignment. I contact the Board of Ed attorney requesting the chance to address the Executive Meeting, and it is denied.

I send my defense to a friend who happens to work in the domestic abuse field. I ask for a character reference and she says, "As CEO, I am not allowed to do that." She says, "Your letter seems sincere."

I am hurt. A friend of 22 years does not say, "I believe you," but says, "the letter seems sincere."

Mona, the incorrigible student, was able to get me on the radar of the administration of my school, able to get me fired and able to get friends to question my character

1ST DAY TO 1ST OBSERVATION (Fall 2022)
*34 school days or 6 weeks & four days

<u>New Systems Learned</u>
I.D. CARD
-getting picture taken and picking up I.D. Card

GENESIS
Gradebook attendance
Gradebook grading
Lesson planner
Marking period grades
Documenting parent phone calls
Posting assignments with grade percentages

NEW BOARD/SMART BOARD
Signing in from lap top (takes 30 second to 2 minutes sometimes)
Posting videos
Posting lesson, notes
Creating slide shows

AESOP
Absence management
PDP/SGO
Observations with my A.P.

OFFICE 365
Emails

TEAMS
How to post lesson, slides, notes, worksheets, etc…

LESSON PLANNER
Posting weekly lessons

COPY MACHINE

There is a shortage of respect and proper compensation for teachers allowing them to actually teach.

Teachers Advocating Against False Accusations -T.A.A.F.A
President & Founder
JamesCGeist50@gmail.com
membership of two – AND growing…

NJEA - NEA - NJ Education Senate Committee – NJ Education Assembly Committee
NJ Dems – NJ GOP - Governor Murphy
12/14/22

Dear Esteemed Members Who Love the Children and Teachers,

Teachers of New Jersey need a law to protect teachers against false allegations.

> *1. The false allegation accuser must immediately be removed from the teacher's class room.*
>
> *2. The student must be expelled from the school.*
>
> *3. Iowa allows a teacher to collect reasonable monetary damages against a plaintiff if the teacher has been found to have been wrongfully accused of improper contact with a student – N.J. should do the same.*

I have been a teacher for 21 years, voted Teacher of the Year in 2012, and have written 28 books you can find on Amazon.com if you type James Curtis Geist into the search engine. I love being a teacher and have often expressed to my parents and wife, my biggest fear is a student with a grievance making a false allegation.

As a former pastor in NYC, I have advocated against sweatshops, child labor, modern day slavery, and genocide in Sudan. I will break my anonymity, I also am a member of a 12 step group – because I believe "the Anonymous People" should advocate for $$ for the treatment of addictions.

My worst fear was realized in mid-November, when <u>several mean girls said to me, "We got our last teacher to quit, and we will get you to quit!"</u> In the meeting with my union reps, the Principal pulled a file with complaints from some students. I was not given the accuser names, but was put on paid leave for two weeks. I was sick of heart, mind. I could not eat or sleep. <u>I WAS SCARED</u>! 6th grade 11 year old girls, willing to destroy the life of teacher, because they did not like the amount of work given in history class. My A.P. said, "Mr. Geist, I love the rigor of your lessons."

The sense of entitlement of these accusers is galling. This is not the generation who grew up during WWII or the Great Depression. They do not understand that many of the poor in the 2/3rds world would love the chance to get a school education. Those who acted in a disrespectful manner in class, did not care about their fellow mates who wanted to learn. My wife who is Filipina agrees. Smart phones and social media contribute to bad manners.

My union and school admin met two weeks later, and the allegations were not even brought up. My written defense with student motivations to rid me was convincing. I also had other adults in my classroom who testified on my behalf. My blood pressure was so high, I had to go to the doctor to adjust my depression medication, and to get a referral to see a cardiologist.

A week later, a father meeting myself, the Principal and a Counselor, slandered my character. The admin never said, "Sorry about the false allegations. Sorry you had to be humiliated by slander from a father." As a non-tenured-teacher, they gave me the pink slip. I was informed 12/9/22 was my lastday working in the Englewood School District. <u>The "mean girls" won – they promised to rid me – and in fact – they won!</u>

If the animals run the zoo, there is no zoo. Anne Sullivan, teacher of Helen Keller said, "Respect first, then learning." When students can make false allegations with no repercussions, school is no longer a safe place.

<u>If there are no consequence for students and their families for false allegations, this will continue to happen to innocent teachers; and you will continue to see more teachers leaving the profession.</u> **N.J. teachers, like in Iowa, must be allowed to sue the child's family and district over false allegations in N.J.** No repercussions equals children continually using false allegations to destroy the lives of teachers.

Thanks for listening. What is the next step? Will you create legislation and support said legislation?

Sincerely,

James C. Geist

Heart-broken and unemployed NJEA member (12/9) as the result of "mean girls" making false allegations.

Chapter 11

Teacher Recovery Work

The Twelve Steps

"The single most important event of the twentieth century was the founding of Alcoholics Anonymous in Akron Ohio in June of 1935" (Burney, p. 9)

<u>The Serenity Prayer</u>.
**God grant me the serenity
to accept the things I cannot change
courage to change the things I can,
and wisdom to know the difference.**
-Christian theologian: Reinhold Niebuhr

Jesus said, "Love your neighbor as you love yourself."

You may love God, but do you love yourself?

Do you love yourself enough to do your inner child work?

Do you love yourself to take care of "unfinished business" (compulsions, false self, ego, the shadow) that may be causing you to self-sabotage your life?

Re-parenting the Self

"Integrity is painful. Without integrity, there can be no wholeness. Integrity requires we be fully open to conflicting forces, ideas and stresses of life" (Peck, Further... p. 192).

"All those who come to the psychotherapist, very few are looking for a conscious level of challenge or an education on discipline. Most are simply seeking relief" (Peck, Road ..., p. 55).

TEN STEPS TO BUILDING IDENTITY

1. Start where you left off developmentally.
2. Bring trustworthy people into your life.
3. Limit your time in environments that are negative.
4. Explore: new foods, activities, clothing, without seeking approval for you choices.
5. Make lots of mistakes.
6. Develop your intuition by asking yourself, not others, what is best for you.
7. Practice gentle boundaries.
8. Express your feelings.
9. Have a clear sense of wants and needs in relationships.
10. BE ALL YOU CAN DO. Embrace your imperfection as something that makes you lovable and unique.

Father Richard Rohr
Father Richard Rohr - St. Anthony's Press

We must climb the tower until age 30,
    when you yearn for more.

The way we have been hurt in childhood,
    we tend to hurt others.

There will be pain when you detach from the ego.

Most people do not do bad things because they are evil, but
    because they are hurting.

God shows up disguised as your life.

Don't project evil on the other because it is diversion from
    keeping the focus on your stuff.

Bumper Sticker:
If you want to heal the world, heal your inner child.

GRIEVING WORK

Al-Anon teaches healthy "detachment." The slogans "Live and let live" and "Let go and let God," free us from the obsession with another person so we can focus on ourselves.

Grieving the loss of a relationship is not unlike grieving a death (75). If someone choses to end a relationship with us, that is their right (81).

No one can take one can take the risk out of life; in a relationship you are offering yourself and you can always be rejected. . .and the chance of being hurt (Berkowitz & Newman 74).

Grief work takes time. When we experience loss, it stirs up energy which needs to be discharged. . .With no release this chronic distress is stored within us as anxiety, fear, anger, resentment, confusion, guilt, emptiness or shame (Whitfield, 85).

Grief work is how we dissolve the body pain .

Jeremiah who wrote Lamentations, was called the "Weeping Prophet." Jesus, fully God, fully man, wept. A fellow pastor who passed, use to say to me when I would get serious, "Jim, learn to dance with the cross you carry."

ANSWER TO YOUR PROBLEMS

In the Big Book of Alcoholics Anonymous, it says, "ACCEPTANCE is the answer to all my problems. When I am disturbed, it is because I find some person, place, thing or situation – some fact of my life – unacceptable to me. I can find no serenity until I accept that person, place, thing or situation as being exactly the way it is suppose to be at this moment. . .<u>Until I accept life completely on life's terms, I cannot be happy.</u> *I need to concentrate no so much on what needs to be changed in the world, as what needs to be changed in my attitudes* (417).

The Gift of Feelings

FEAR is the gift of wisdom and freedom.

ANGER is the gift of strength an protectiveness.

SADNESS is healing and empathy.

GUILT is the gift of the ability to see we have impact on others.

SHAME is the bedrock of honor.

JOY is nurturing, health and healing.

HOPE is a positive push toward a belief in betterment and a brighter future.

HOW TO BECOME YOUR OWN BEST FRIEND
Mildred Newman & Bernard Berkowitz

We are not born with the secret how to live, and too many never learn it...The source is not outside us; it is within. We must realize the kingdom is within us; we already have the key...We must take responsibility for our lives (22).

We have to use everything we got - feelings, intuition, intelligence and our will power (45).

It is an awful blow to feel you have made a mistake. This is why most people don't want to change. It would mean admitting you were wrong (51).

To be abandoned as a child is a terrifying experience...but as an adult, aloneness is quite different. He needs it to grow and to get to know himself and his powers. Someone who cannot tolerate aloneness is someone who does not know he is grown up (56).

The secret to living is to come to life. We can learn to become our own best friend. If we do, we have a friend for life. We can buoy ourselves comfort and sustenance the times when there is no one else (90).

RELATIONSHIP BILL OF RIGHTS

You have the right to...
...to put yourself first sometimes.
...to be the final judge of your feelings.
...to your own opinions and convictions.
...to say NO.
...to be alone, even if the other would prefer your company.
...to not take responsibility for someone else's problem.

It is never your responsibility to...
...to give what your really don't want to give.
...drain your strength for others
...follow the crowd.
...feel guilty about inner desires.
...be anyone but <u>exactly</u> who you are.

Feminist X (part II) by James C. Geist circa 2014

She could work from home three days a week, but she lived at my place five days a week with her Boston Terrier named Ellie, after Eleanor Roosevelt. I had the summer off as a teacher, and feeling off-center, I said, I need to go to a meeting – of the 12 step kind. The girlfriend said, "What will I do the next three hours?" Incredulous, I made the following suggestions:

>Nap
>Watch a movie
>Take the dog for a walk
>Read a book
>Sun bathe on the deck
>Go for a hike,
>Have a campfire
>Mow the lawn
>Vacuum the house
>Wash the house windows
>Call some family and friends
>Change the oil in the car
>Write a letter to a Congressman
>Write a poem
>Go for a run
>Do the laundry
>Stain the shed
>Search the google machine and type in "things to do."
>Work on a peace plan for the world.

I am shocked by my feminist girlfriend's codependency. As I drive to the meeting, I listen to Rodriguez, "Woman be gone, you have stayed too long."

The Power of Now by Eckhart Tolle

Incessant mental noise prevents you from inner stillness with Being. It creates the false self and casts a shadow of fear and suffering. When you believe you are your mind, that is a delusion. You are not "the thinker "(17).

When you obsessing, become "the witness," see yourself above your thinking. To the ego, the present hardly exists. It always wants to keep the past alive to continue its survival (26).

The mind unconsciously loves problems because it gives you an identity of sorts. . .You become so overwhelmed, you lose your life, of Being (41).

Wherever you are, be totally there. Live in the Now. Live in the Present. You will even learn how to enjoy your own company – joy in the self (53).

ACOA RECOVERY: HOW WILL I KNOW IF I AM RECOVERING?

1. I accept myself fully. I have a basic self-love and self-regard.

2. I accept others as they are without trying to change them.

3. I validate myself rather than searching for a relationship to give me a sense of self-worth.

4. I do not need to be needed to feel worthy. I am s special just being. I need not "do."

5. When a relationship is destructive, I am able to let go of it without suffering disabling depression.

6. I value my own serenity above all else. I am protective of myself and my well-being.

7. I know that a relationship, in order to work, must be between parties, who each have a capacity for intimacy.

St. Joseph ACOA Rutherford NJ

Affirmations & Quotes

I accept pain as my teacher.

I comfort and nurture myself.

Time is a transforming my loneliness into solitude, my suffering into meaning, and relationships into intimacy.

I commit to reality at all costs, knowing that is where I will find serenity.

I accept life is difficult and that leaning into the struggle adds to my balance.

POSTIVE AFFIRMATIONS
Codependents Anonymous 1988

I am a child of God.
I am a precious and worthwhile person.
I am beautiful on the inside and outside.
I love myself unconditionally.
I can allow myself leisure time without feeling guilty.
I deserve to be loved by myself and others.
I am loved, because I deserve love.

I forgive myself for hurting myself and others.
I forgive myself for letting others hurt me.

I am not alone, I am one with God and the universe.
I am whole and good.
I am enough.
I am not perfect, but I am excellent.

Affirmations

I allow others to take responsibility for their lives.
I am grateful for a sense of humor
I have the courage to change.
I take risks that will help me grow in a positive, healthy ways.
I value my emotion that I get to know, understand and love more each day.

Quotes

Quotes for Reflection

How does one become a butterfly? You must want to fly so much, you are willing to give up being a caterpillar.
-Cecil Selig

There's only one corner of the universe you can be certain of improving, and that is your own self.
-Roderick Thorp

Do not wish it was easier, wish you were better. Don't wish for fewer problems, wish for mor skills. Don't wish for less challenges, wish for more wisdom.
-Earl Shoaf

It takes courage to grow up and become who you really are.
-E.E. Cummings

Watch your thoughts, they become words. Words become actions. Actions become habits. Habits become character. Character becomes your destiny. As we think, we become.

In the first half of life, we fight the devil; the second half God.

Holding unto anger is like grasping a hot coal with the intent of throwing it at someone else; and you are the one who gets burned.

Don't wait for the rain to pass; learn to dance in the rain.

Charles Bukowski in his poem, **'Love is a Dog from Hell,** says…

"There is a loneliness in the world so great. . . people mutilated either by love or no love, people no good to each other. . . we are afraid. . .our educational system has not told us of the terror of one person aching in one place so alone."

The End

Cell Phone Addiction

We have a cell phone addiction in our schools.

In the classroom are Smart Boards, laptops and cell phones. Teachers get judged on 32 categories via the Danielson Rubric. How is a teacher to compete against addiction?

In my Black History class, the boss complains there is not enough engagement. I ask if I can smash cell phones with a hammer and I am told "no." My job is to teach, not to be the cell phone and ear bud police.

Al-anon teaches "healthy detachment," meaning you allow a person to suffer the consequences of his/her decisions. Cell phone addicts cannot get help until they first admit they have a problem.

My suggestion is cell phones be collected by school security at the beginning of the day and handed back the end of the day. In NYC, there use to be cell phone vehicle, a phone library if you will, parked in front of school for $1 fee per day.

Phones and social media have increased mental-stress, self-injurious behavior and suicidal intentions among our kids. Why don't school boards, administrations and teacher unions support a ban on cellphones during the school day?

Our students need to learn how to live in the present. Do not be naïve, there will be no true engagement in class until phones are locked away. This is just one of many reasons teachers are leaving the profession today.

Ring, ring – gotta go! Just kidding ; as an aside, I have never owned cell phone, and I am still alive.

James Curtis Geist Biography

James Curtis Geist has been a public school teacher for over twenty-one years. This book is filled with funny and poignant anecdotes of working as a teacher in the nutty-marvelous world of a classroom. The book takes a look at the challenges and pulse of life of public school life in the 21st century. Subjects include perfectionism, substitute teacher life, bosses, stories of students, childhood school day flashbacks, sexual harassment, guns, covid, terrorism, unions and false accusations.

This is about a thoughtful teacher contemplating public school challenges and solutions. Suffering brings change teaching us to become better human beings and teachers. This is a life story in education is full of wit, warmth and wisdom, and will also make you laugh.

This book also delves into one of the greatest fears of any teacher; a student with a grievance making a false accusation, because they can. This book shares James' experience in the fall of 2022 in suburban N.J. school district, because a group of mean girls did not like him. Why are there no legal consequences for young people who do so? What are teacher unions doing to protect their rank-n-file? Why is this allowed to continue in 2023?

This the 29th book written by Geist. He has written an autobiography, books for children, young adults, history, and poetry and anecdotes. James has taught in N.Y.C., Newark, Jersey City, and a few charter schools.

James lives in the woods of northern New Jersey with his wife and stepson. He is not related to Bill, Willie or Ken Geist, all authors, but wishes he was to take advantage of the nepotism connections.

INDEX

What Teachers Do……………………...………..25
Perfectionism……………………………………26
Codependency……………………………………27
Stages of Life……………………………….......29
Teacher Movies……………………….………..31

Roll Call………………..34, 53, 85, 110, 172, 185
Prank Names……………35, 54, 86, 117, 173, 186

Subbing…………………………………………37
Unisex Bathroom………………………….…..43
Schools: 1950 vs. 2010…………………………45
Education in the Philippines……………..……..56
Service………………………………………….57

Principle or Principal……………………………51
Candy Crush……………………………………59
Teacher Lunch Room……………………………61
Fire Drills………………………………………62
Headaches………………………………………63

Student Fights……………………..……...……64
Retirement…………………………….………...65
Bed Bugs………………………………………..67
Commute to Work……………………………….69
Teacher Summer House Painters………………71

Holidays………………………………………...75
Parking Lot………………………………..……76
Tired……………………………………………81
Gov. Christie – health care……………………..83
Student Lunchroom……………………………..87

Index page 2

Juvenile Delinquent..............................88
Crazy Student...................................89
Mr. Incredible..................................91
Cannot Read Clocks..............................98
The "N" word....................................94

Nurses Office..................................104
Mom's to black son.............................105
Class Quite....................................107
Acting White...................................108
Helen's Keller's Teacher.......................110

Student Failure................................113
Education by Decades...........................118
Stages of Life.................................120
Cell Phones...............................310, 123
Innocents in Jail..............................126

School Prayer..................................128
Suffrage.......................................131
Councilman Martinez............................132
Dignity..134
Charter Schools................................135

Evening School.................................137
Solution to Education..........................139
Good Master....................................142
Blame the Teacher..............................143
A Teacher Dies.................................146

Philadelphia - 1977............................157
Class of 1984..................................158
Printing Class.................................161

Index page 3

My Favorite Jobs.............................166
Discovery..168
Social Pyramids..............................177
Zombies..183
Time Flies.......................................187

School Closing................................188
Solidarity..189
J.C. Lockdown................................190
Depression......................................192
Pink Slips..193

Danielson Rubric.............................195
COVID..198
Vaccinations...................................200
Masks...204
Health Insurance.............................206

Guns...209
Racism..212
Post Traumatic Stress Disorder......217
Constant Change of Technology....219
Cell Phones....................................224
Humility...225

Codependency................................228
Central Park Five............................229
9/11 Attack..............................241-263
T.A.A.F.A.......................................292
Biography.......................................310
School Yard UFO Visits.................315

School Yard U.F.O. Encounters

At one of my campfires in 2004, Kathleen C., shared with me a story about when she was in elementary school in Passaic County New Jersey (late 1960's), a U.F.O. landed in the playground, and little people were witnessed. She was a credible friend, and I believed her. Her school held an assembly, and some men from the government told the children to keep the story hush, hush – which many did.

In 2021, **I purchased the book School Yard UFO Encounters, by Preston Dennett**, longtime UFO researcher and frequent guest on U.F.O. television programs. He documents over 100 cases in the book.

For the past 170 years, schools across the United States and world have been targeted and visited by Unidentified Ariel Phenomena (since the U.S. Government has admitted to such things in 2019). They should be called A.E F.V.'s for Alternative Energy Flying Vehicles. Image if we could tap into this cheap energy and no more gasoline?

These school yard visits are not just fly overs, in many cases, the objects hover over the school for long periods at low elevation. The vehicles sometimes land in the school yard at elementary, middle schools, high schools and colleges.

In 2016, Dr. Roger Stankovic, "Over the past 50 years, UFO's have appeared in broad daylight sporadically at various school yards over four continents around the world."

The top four sightings are listed as:

1. Westhall High School in Victoria Australia (4-6-1966) *200 plus witnesses.

2. Broad Haven Primary School in Haverfordwest, South Wales (2-4-1977). *14 witnesses.

3. Crestwood Elementary in Opa-locka, Florida on (4-7-1967) *200 witnesses.

4. Ariel School, Ruwa Zimbabwe, Africa (9-16-1994) *62 witnesses.

Why is this subject not being taken more seriously?

Why is this not taught in schools?

Why are these stories not front page news?

Coral Lorenzo said, "Children are definitely less subject to dogmatic or pre-conceived notions than adults. Perhaps the visitors hope that exhibitions over schools will influence the population to some extent."

Shannon Quinn says, "True believers think that young school children are less threatening to aliens, so it makes them easier to approach with their messages from beyond the galaxy."

Another interesting fact about the visitations, while most U.F.O. sightings are brief, **school yard visitations are not brief.** Many last for many minutes to hours and in some cases take place over a series of days.

Why do the extraterrestrials express such a profound interest in our children? What is the agenda?
can tell you this, I wish they would abduct my bosses– it would make my life more manageable. I just hope my bosses are not probed where the sun don't shine.

Made in the USA
Middletown, DE
07 January 2023

20255628R00176